SHORT WALKS DARTMOOR SOUTH
IVYBRIDGE AND PRINCETOWN

by Steve Davison

One of the stone rows at Drizzlecombe (Walk 9)

CONTENTS

Using this guide.. 4
Route summary table 6
Map key 7
Introduction.. 9
   Walking in South Dartmoor 10
   Where to stay... 11
   Travel 11

The walks

1.	Double Waters	13
2.	Great Staple Tor and Windy Post Cross	17
3.	Four Winds	23
4.	Princetown and King's Tor	27
5.	Princetown and Nun's Cross	33
6.	Crockern Tor and Wistman's Wood	41
7.	Devonport Leat and Crazy Well Pool..........................	45
8.	Meavy and Sheepstor..	51
9.	Ditsworthy and Drizzlecombe	59
10.	Ivybridge and Henlake Down	63
11.	Butterdon Hill and Western Beacon	69
12.	South Brent and Shipley Bridge..................................	73
13.	Dartmeet tors	79
14.	Holne and Leigh Tor	83
15.	Ten Commandments Stone...	89

Useful information 95

SHORT WALKS DARTMOOR — SOUTH

USING THIS GUIDE

Routes in this book

In this book you will find a selection of easy or moderate walks suitable for almost everyone, including casual walkers and families with children, or for when you only have a short time to fill. The routes have been carefully chosen to allow you to explore the area and its attractions. Most routes are circular or out-and-back, although some linear walks may be included that use public transport to get back to the start. Although there may be some climbs there is no challenging terrain, but do bear in mind that conditions can sometimes be wet or muddy underfoot. A route summary table is included on page 6 to help you choose the right walk.

Clothing and footwear

You won't need any special equipment to enjoy these walks. The weather in Britain can be changeable, so choose clothing suitable for the season and wear or carry a waterproof jacket. For footwear, comfortable walking boots or trainers with a good grip are best. A small rucksack for drinks, snacks and spare clothing is useful. See www.adventuresmart.uk.

Walk descriptions

At the beginning of each walk you'll find all the information you need:

- start/finish location, with postcode and a what3words address to help you find it
- parking and transport information, estimated walking time, total distance and climb
- details of public toilets available along the route and where you can get refreshments
- a summary of the key highlights of the walk and what you might see

Timings given are the time to complete the walk at a reasonable walking pace. Allow extra time for extended stops or if walking with children.

The route is described in clear, easy-to-follow directions, with each waypoint marked on an accompanying map extract. It's a good idea to read the whole of the route instructions before setting out, so that you know what to expect.

Maps, GPX files and what3words

Extracts from the OS® 1:25,000 map accompany each route. GPX files for all the walks in this book are available to download at www.cicerone.co.uk/1192/gpx.

What3words is a free smartphone app which identifies every 3m square of the globe with a unique three-word address, e.g. ///destiny.cafe.sonic. For more information see https://what3words.com/products/what3words-app.

USING THIS GUIDE

Walking with children

Even young children can be surprisingly strong walkers, but every family is different and you may need to adapt the timings given in this book to take that into account. Make sure you go at the pace of the slowest member and choose a walk with an exciting objective in mind, such as a cave, river, waterfall or picnic spot. Many of the walks can be shortened to suit – suggestions are included at the end of the route description.

Dogs

Sheep or cattle may be found grazing on a number of these walks. Keep dogs under control at all times so that they don't scare or disturb livestock or wildlife. Cattle, particularly cows with calves, may very occasionally pose a risk to walkers with dogs. If you ever feel threatened by cattle, you should let go of your dog's lead and let it run free.

Enjoying the countryside responsibly

Enjoy the countryside and treat it with respect to protect our natural environments. Stick to footpaths and take your litter home with you. When driving, slow down on rural roads and park considerately, or better still use public transport. For more details check out www.gov.uk/countryside-code.

The Countryside Code

Respect everyone
- be considerate to those living in, working in and enjoying the countryside
- leave gates and property as you find them
- do not block access to gateways or driveways when parking
- be nice, say hello, share the space
- follow local signs and keep to marked paths unless wider access is available

Protect the environment
- take your litter home – leave no trace of your visit
- do not light fires and only have BBQs where signs say you can
- always keep dogs under control and in sight
- dog poo – bag it and bin it – any public waste bin will do
- care for nature – do not cause damage or disturbance

Enjoy the outdoors
- check your route and local conditions
- plan your adventure – know what to expect and what you can do
- enjoy your visit, have fun, make a memory

SHORT WALKS DARTMOOR — SOUTH

ROUTE SUMMARY TABLE

WALK NAME	START POINT	TIME
1. Double Waters	Bedford Bridge	2½hr
2. Great Staple Tor and Windy Post Cross	Pork Hill car park	1¾hr
3. Four Winds	Four Winds car park	2hr
4. Princetown and King's Tor	Princetown	3hr
5. Princetown and Nun's Cross	Princetown	2¾hr
6. Crockern Tor and Wistman's Wood	Two Bridges	2hr
7. Devonport Leat and Crazy Well Pool	Norsworthy Bridge	2hr
8. Meavy and Sheepstor	Meavy	2½hr
9. Ditsworthy and Drizzlecombe	Gutter Tor car park	2hr
10. Ivybridge and Henlake Down	Ivybridge	1½hr
11. Butterdon Hill and Western Beacon	Ivybridge railway station	3hr
12. South Brent and Shipley Bridge	South Brent	3¼hr
13. Dartmeet tors	Dartmeet	2hr
14. Holne and Leigh Tor	Holne	2¾hr
15. Ten Commandments Stone	Cold East Cross	2hr

MAP KEY

DISTANCE	HIGHLIGHTS
7.5km (4¾ miles)	Woodland, riverside, former railway
5.5km (3½ miles)	Tors, leat, wayside cross
6.5km (4 miles)	Prehistoric relics, tor, views
11km (6¾ miles)	Quarries, tor, old railway track
9.5km (6 miles)	Wayside cross, leat, infamous mire
7km (4¼ miles)	Woodland, tors, views
7km (4¼ miles)	Woodland, leat, pool, views
7.5km (4¾ miles)	Pretty villages, pub, reservoir
6.5km (4 miles)	Film location, prehistoric relics, old tin mine
5km (3 miles)	Woodland, riverside and heathland
9.5km (6 miles)	Former tramway, prehistoric relics, views
9.5km (6 miles)	Village, open moor, views
5.5km (3½ miles)	Open moor, tors, views
8.5km (5¼ miles)	Village, riverside, woodland, open moor, tor, views
6.5km (4 miles)	Fascinating memorial, tors, views

SYMBOLS USED ON ROUTE MAPS

S Start point

F Finish point

SF Start and finish at the same place

 Waypoint

Route line

MAPPING IS SHOWN AT A SCALE OF 1:25,000

0 KM — 0.25 — 0.5
0 miles — 0.25

DOWNLOAD THE GPX FILES FOR FREE AT
www.cicerone.co.uk/1192/gpx

The view from Buckland Beacon (Walk 15)

INTRODUCTION

The tree-shaded River Meavy (Walk 7)

Dartmoor, a national park since 1951, is a wild, and at times isolated, upland area tucked in the south-western corner of Devon, in south-west England. It is a land of blanket bogs, grass moors dotted with fascinating tors, tumbling streams crossed by old stone clapper bridges, and a diverse range of wildlife. Several millennia ago our ancestors left behind a fascinating treasure trove, from intriguing stone rows to ancient stone circles, burial cairns and hut circles. But there are also the stark ruins of Dartmoor's mining heritage, and picturesque villages and hamlets that are home to cosy pubs and historic buildings.

Yes, the weather can be inclement at times, low cloud and mist can obscure the views and the high rainfall leads to numerous bogs and mires, but this climate also brings with it fascinating woodlands clothed in moss and lichen like some enchanted land. When the mist rolls in, the tors take on an other-worldly character – it was here that Sir Arthur Conan Doyle gained inspiration for his Sherlock Holmes novel *The Hound of the Baskervilles*.

Great Mis Tor (Walk 3)

Walking in South Dartmoor

The area covered by this guide encompasses the southern half of Dartmoor, roughly anywhere south of a line drawn from Tavistock in the west to Heathfield near Newton Abbot in the east. The walks are designed to show the varied nature of Dartmoor, from the high open moors dotted with craggy tors to tranquil woodland and riverside paths. Some of the walks follow sections of two long-distance routes: the Dartmoor Way and the Two Moors Way.

The routes are generally well signposted except on the open moor, and they all follow fairly well-used paths. They can be enjoyed all year round; however, some of the paths may be wet and muddy, especially during the winter months, and some of the walks have streams to cross with no footbridges. The temperature and weather can change quickly on the open moor, so it is always a good idea to carry some extra clothing, including a waterproof jacket, just in case.

The walks, which are all circular, explore many interesting places across southern Dartmoor, including Great Staple Tor (Walk 2); the fascinating ancient relics at Merrivale (Walk 3) and Drizzlecombe (Walk 9); the rare temperate rainforest of Wistman's Wood (Walk 6); the Ten Commandments Stone (Walk 15); and picturesque villages such as Meavy (Walk 8) and Holne (Walk 14). There is also a more challenging route (Walk 12) from South Brent.

The joys of walking on Dartmoor are many. Sit for a while atop a craggy tor and admire the views while listening to nature's music, from skylarks singing high above to the wind whispering over the moor. Look for wildlife, enjoy a picnic, or explore the ancient sites and wonder as to their purpose. But most of all, enjoy and respect the unique landscape, character and wildlife of Dartmoor.

Where to stay

There is a wide range of accommodation across Dartmoor, from campsites to pubs with rooms and hotels, both within and outside the national park.

The main bases in the southern half of the national park that offer a range of facilities – such as shops, pubs and accommodation – are Ashburton, Buckfastleigh, Horrabridge, Princetown and Yelverton. Outside the national park there are several larger towns, including Ivybridge, Newton Abbott and Totnes (all offering rail services), Bovey Tracey and Tavistock.

Travel

The most useful railway stations for reaching the southern half of Dartmoor are Exeter, Newton Abbot, Totnes, Ivybridge and Plymouth, with good connections to London, South Wales, the Midlands and the North. There are no train stations within Dartmoor National Park.

Several of the walks in this guidebook start at, or near, public transport links, as detailed in the walk information. Useful bus services include Exeter to Ivybridge via Ashburton and South Brent; Plymouth to Tavistock via Yelverton and Meavy; and Tavistock and Yelverton to Princetown and Two Bridges. There are also more local bus services, but these may be quite infrequent.

If travelling by car, Dartmoor is within easy reach of the M5 motorway in Devon via the A30 along the northern edge, and the A38 along the eastern and southern edge; joining these along the western edge is the A386. The B3212 crosses Dartmoor from Dunsford to Yelverton; another route crosses from Ashburton to Tavistock. Extending off these is a network of narrow lanes, often with passing places.

The speed limit on all parts of the open moor is 40mph, reducing to 30mph in places. On the open moor, ponies, sheep and cattle roam freely so extra care is required, especially at night. All accidents with stock animals must be reported to the Livestock Protection Officer (see 'Useful information'). Only park in designated car parks or where on-street parking is allowed, and never block access points.

Chimney from the 19th-century West Down copper mine

WALK 1
Double Waters

Start/finish	Bedford Bridge, just west of Horrabridge
Locate	///variation.boarding.scenes
Cafes/pubs	Pub at Horrabridge (1km off route)
Transport	Buses from Plymouth and Tavistock stop on the A386 at Bedford Bridge (150m from the start)
Parking	Drake's Trail car park at Bedford Bridge (PL20 7RZ)
Toilets	No public toilets on route

Time 2½hr
Distance 7.5km (4¾ miles)
Climb 200m

Woodland and riverside walking, an impressive viaduct and old mine workings

From Bedford Bridge the route heads up through woods before joining the Dartmoor Way and briefly following the Drake's Trail along a former railway. After heading down to Grenofen Bridge it's off alongside the River Walkham to Double Waters, where the River Walkham joins the River Tavy. The return route climbs up the south side of the valley and down through woodland back to Bedford Bridge.

Following the Dartmoor Way towards Grenofen Bridge

SHORT WALKS DARTMOOR — SOUTH

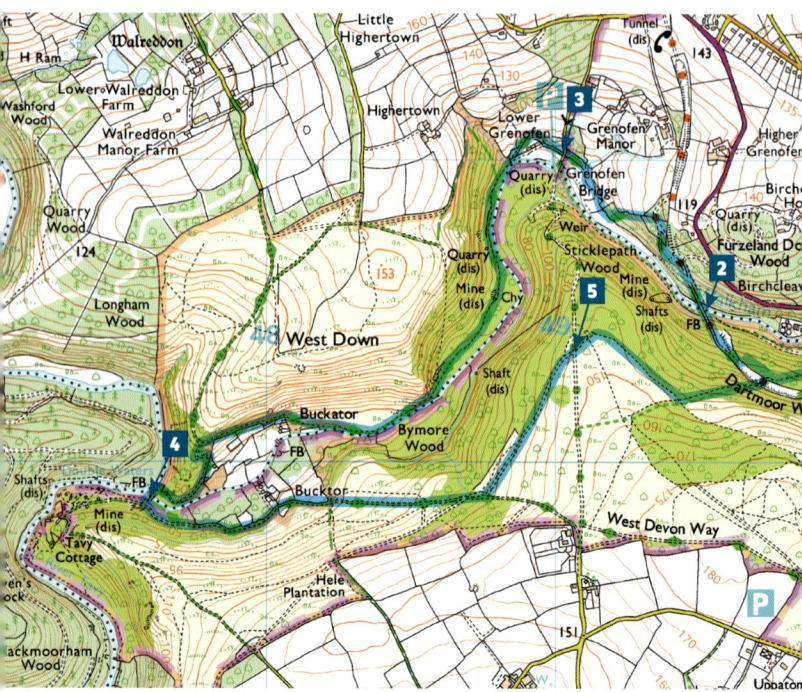

1 At **Bedford Bridge** head away from the A386 to the back of the car park and take the waymarked path, soon crossing a bridge over a stream. Continue through the trees to a signed junction. Fork left uphill and just before a bridge over the former railway, turn right on a narrow path. Shortly afterwards bear left to join the former railway track that now forms the Drake's Trail. Turn right and shortly cross Gem Bridge over the **River Walkham**. The walk now follows the Dartmoor Way to Double Waters.

2 Continue along the Drake's Trail as it crosses another bridge and, as the route swings right, turn left through a small gate with a Dartmoor Way waymark. Head down through the trees to the bottom and bear right along an enclosed path. Then go through a gate to a lane. To the left is **Grenofen Bridge** and the River Walkham. For a

WALK 1 – DOUBLE WATERS

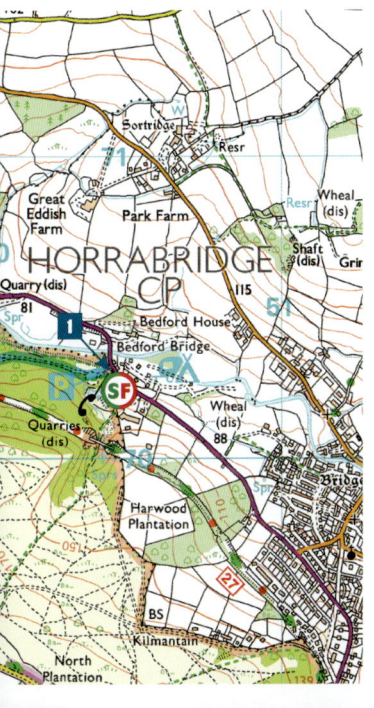

shorter route turn left to cross the bridge.

3 Cross straight over the lane and follow the driveway opposite, before forking right to follow the bridleway behind the buildings at **Lower Grenofen**. Continue along the wooded valley, with the River Walkham on your left, later passing a stone chimney. The chimney was part of the 19th-century West Down copper mine. On reaching a stone wall on the left, the route heads uphill away from the river, passes to the right of a building (**Buckator**) and then continues along the track. At a signed track junction, turn left downhill and then follow the river again. Keep to the path as it heads up between the two rock stacks of Goat Rock, before bearing left to the footbridge at **Double Waters**. Here the River Walkham joins the River Tavy.

The River Walkham after passing Grenofen Bridge

4 Cross the footbridge, keep ahead up to a track and turn left along it. After passing a house (**Bucktor**), the track is tarred and rises more steeply. Keep ahead until you reach the edge of the wood on your left. Turn left along a wide grassy track, keeping the trees over to your left, to reach a crossing track.

5 Cross half-left and continue past bushes, soon curving to the right, and continue to a cross-junction. Turn left down through the trees. Cross the bridge over the former railway and retrace the route down to a junction passed earlier. Turn right and follow the path back towards **Bedford Bridge**.

– To shorten
At Waypoint 3 turn left across Grenofen Bridge and follow the track steeply uphill to a crossing route at Waypoint 5 (just after leaving the trees) and turn left. This shortens the walk by 3.5km (1hr).

+ To lengthen
At the gate in Waypoint 2 continue along the Drake's Trail to the 400m-long Grenofen Tunnel, then retrace your steps and go through the gate to continue the route. This adds just over 1km (20min).

Drake's Trail and Gem Bridge

The Drake's Trail, a 34km walking and cycling route between Tavistock and Plymouth (which forms part of the NCN 27), follows the line of the former South Devon & Tavistock Railway. The railway, which opened in 1859, was closed in 1962 and three years later the 15-span Walkham Viaduct over the River Walkham was demolished. Jump forward to 2012 and a new 200m-long bridge, known as the Gem Bridge, was opened to complete the Drake's Trail. The trail itself is named after Sir Francis Drake, who was born near Tavistock and later purchased Buckland Abbey.

Easy walking on the way back towards Bedford Bridge

WALK 2
Great Staple Tor and Windy Post Cross

Time 1¾hr
Distance 5.5km (3½ miles)
Climb 190m

A walk visiting tors with views, a leat and an ancient wayside cross

Start/finish	Pork Hill car park
Locate	///keener.youngest.seducing
Cafes/pubs	Occasional ice cream van at the car park, pub at Merrivale (1.25km off route)
Transport	Buses from Tavistock, Plymouth, Exeter and Yelverton stop at Merrivale on the B3357 (1.5km from start)
Parking	Pork Hill car park (PL19 9JU) on the B3357, 5km east of Tavistock
Toilets	No public toilets on route

From Pork Hill the route makes a steady climb up to Cox Tor. After admiring the views, it's a relatively easy walk across a saddle to visit the impressive granite rock stacks on Great Staple Tor. After passing Middle Staple Tor, head downhill to cross the B3357. Then it's a level walk alongside a leat to reach the picturesque Windy Post Cross. The last section is a gentle walk over Whitchurch Common back to Pork Hill.

The wide path heading up Cox Tor

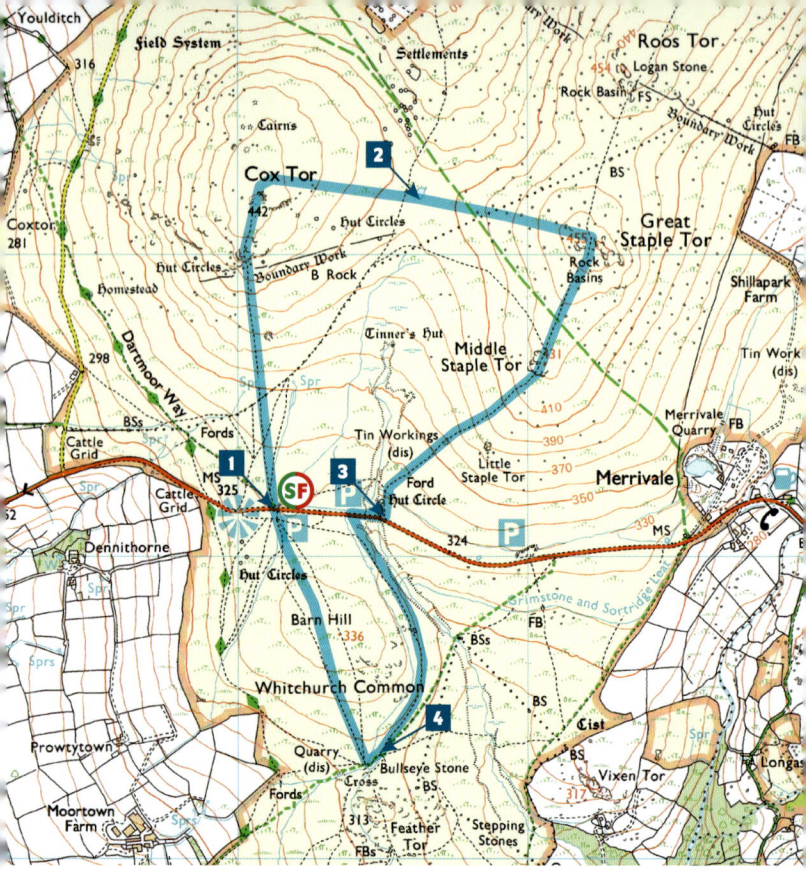

1 From the entrance to Park Hill **car park** cross the B3357 and follow the wide, grassy path uphill. Later pick your way up the boulder-strewn slope to the trig point on **Cox Tor** (442m). Continue beyond the trig point for a few paces and then turn right down the grassy slope to the saddle and a pond. The pond might be dry in the summer.

Cox Tor offers great views. Looking towards the Princetown TV mast and rotating clockwise there is King's Tor, then Pew Tor, further round is Cornwall and Bodmin Moor, then the distinctive outline of Brent Tor and its church. Further round still are the high tops above Okehampton, then Roos Tor, Great Staple Tor and Great Mis Tor.

WALK 2 – GREAT STAPLE TOR AND WINDY POST CROSS

2 Pass to the right of the pond and keep ahead up towards the granite stacks and outcrops that make up **Great Staple Tor** (455m). Turn right, passing between two of the large rock stacks, and then continue over open ground to **Middle Staple Tor** (431m), keeping ahead at a crossing bridleway.

> To visit the pub at Merrivale, turn left down the bridleway to a fence above Merrivale Quarry and turn right (quarry on your left) down to join the B3357. Turn left down the road to the pub. Retrace your steps to continue the walk. This diversion adds 2.5km, 130m climbing and 1hr to the walk.

Once past the tor, bear half-right down the boulder-strewn slope, aiming for a small parking area to the left of the main Pork Hill car park. The route becomes clearer as you descend. On nearing a wide stream gully (with old tin workings), bear left down to the road (B3357).

3 Turn right alongside the road, crossing the stream gully, then turn left across the road and continue uphill slightly. Just before a narrow stream ahead, turn left to leave the road. Alternatively, for a shorter walk keep ahead. Head across the grass, with the stream over to your right. Soon the Grimstone and Sortridge Leat appears on your left. Follow the leat as it curves clockwise round the hill to a footbridge. On the way, look out for the abandoned granite millstone beside the leat.

> ⓘ *Buckfast Abbey, founded by King Canute in 1018, became a ruin following Henry VIII's Dissolution of the Monasteries. Exiled French monks rebuilt the Abbey Church in the 20th century (www.buckfast.org.uk).*

Looking east from Cox Tor

SHORT WALKS DARTMOOR — SOUTH

4 Do not cross the footbridge but keep ahead, with the leat on your left, to reach a **stone cross** (which is to the left across the leat). Known as Windy Post (or Beckamoor) Cross, this well-preserved medieval wayside cross, stands on the ancient route between the abbeys at Tavistock and Buckfast. Now turn right and head over **Whitchurch Common**, crossing Barn Hill (336m) on the way – there are a few paths heading in the same general direction and leading back to the **car park**.

– To shorten
At Waypoint 3 continue alongside the road back to Pork Hill car park. This reduces the walk by 1.5km (30min).

+ To lengthen
On reaching Great Staple Tor turn left down to a dip and then up to Roos Tor (454m), another lovely viewpoint. Retrace your steps to continue the route from Great Staple Tor. This adds 1km (20min).

Large granite stacks on Great Staple Tor

Grimstone and Sortridge Leat

The Grimstone and Sortridge Leat, which starts from Grimstone Head Weir on the River Walkham to the north of Merrivale, was constructed to provide water to the medieval manors of Grimstone and Sortridge (with branches to several farms). The Bullseye Stone, seen on this walk beside the Windy Post Cross, is a stone with a circular hole through it. It is placed across the leat channel so that only a limited amount of water is diverted from the main channel.

Old millstone beside the Grimstone and Sortridge Leat

One of the double stone rows at Merrivale

WALK 3
Four Winds

Start/finish	*Four Winds car park*
Locate	*///subsystem.soap.info*
Cafes/pubs	*Pub at Merrivale (600m off route)*
Transport	*Buses from Tavistock, Plymouth, Exeter and Yelverton stop at Merrivale on the B3357*
Parking	*Four Winds car park (PL20 6ST) on the B3357 near Merrivale*
Toilets	*No public toilets on route*

A walk of two halves that can easily be undertaken as two separate, shorter walks. Explore the fascinating prehistoric sites of Merrivale on a fairly level walk and then climb to the top of Great Mis Tor for a wonderful view before retracing your route back down. Great Mis Tor lies outside the Merrivale Firing Range; however, if the red flag is flying, then the range is in use and you must not stray any further beyond the tor.

Time 2hr
Distance 6.5km (4 miles)
Climb 205m

A walk of contrasts, with fascinating prehistoric Merrivale, extensive views from Great Mis Tor and a great pub nearby

Little Mis Tor

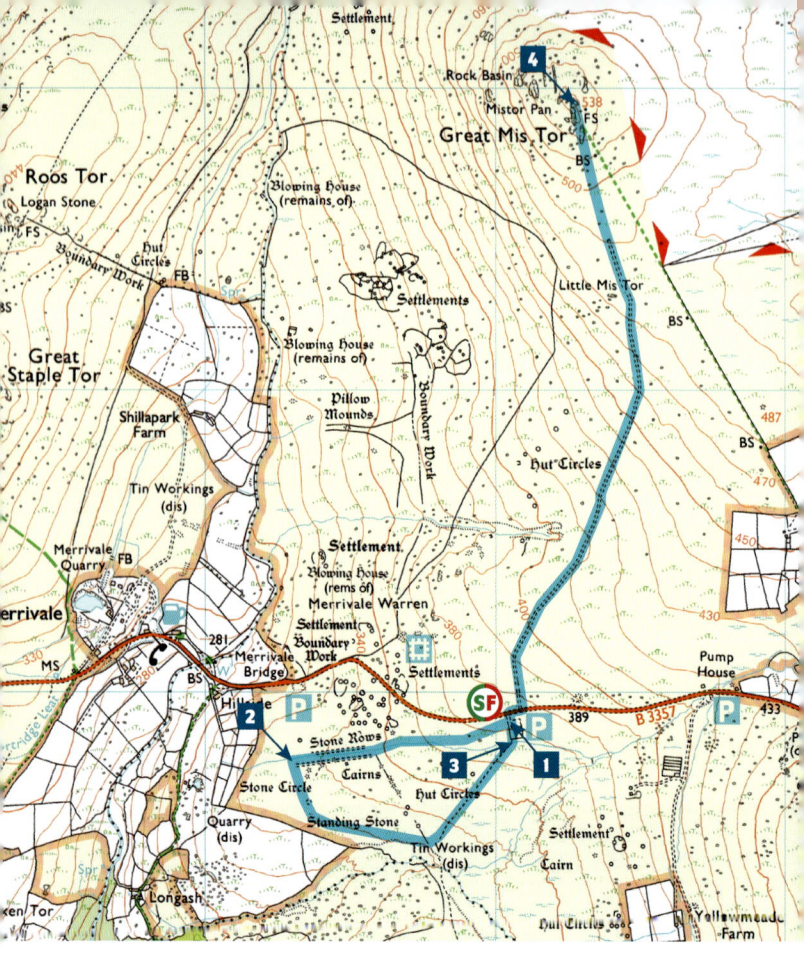

1 Head to the top left corner of the **car park** nearest to the road and immediately after the wall ends on your left, turn left. Follow the grassy path, soon with a stream on your left and the road some distance to the right. On nearing the stone rows, cross the single slab footbridge over the stream and continue, soon passing between the two double **stone rows**, with the stream and one of the stone rows on your right. Head to a path junction at the far end of the left-hand stone row and turn left.

WALK 3 – FOUR WINDS

To visit the Dartmoor Inn at Merrivale, at the end of the stone row turn right, cross the bridge over the stream and bear half-left to reach the B3557. Turn left down alongside the road to the pub on the right. Retrace your steps to rejoin the route (25min there and back).

2 Follow the grassy path gently downhill to pass a stone circle and continue to the tall **standing stone**, or menhir. From here there are several paths. Take the second path to the left, aiming for the large TV mast on North Hessary Tor (the first left leads directly back to Four Winds). Over to your right is a wall at first and then a stream with old tin workings. At the path junction turn half-left towards the trees, passing a boundary stone along the way. Cross a clapper bridge and go through the squeeze gap into the **car park**.

3 Continue through the car park to the B3357 and turn right alongside the road for 50m. Then turn left across the road and take the track opposite. Follow this uphill to **Little Mis Tor**, where the main track ends at a turning area. Keep ahead up a path to the granite outcrops of **Great Mis Tor** (538m), with wonderful views.

Facing the tall TV mast near Princetown and moving right (clockwise) you can see Plymouth Sound, while further round is Cornwall and then the high tors of Northern Dartmoor. On the main outcrop, just north of the flagpole, is a fine example of a rock basin known as the Mistor Pan.

Approaching the clapper bridge and squeeze gap at Four Winds

4 After admiring the views, turn around and retrace your steps back down to the Four Winds **car park**.

> ⓘ *Four Winds was originally the site of Foggintor School, built for quarry worker's children. The perimeter walls still stand among the trees.*

− To shorten

The walk can easily be split into two shorter walks both starting from Four Winds. The Merrivale loop is 2km (30min) and fairly level; the Great Mis Tor loop, which involves some climbing, is 4.5km (90min).

Merrivale

The cist with split lid at Merrivale

Dartmoor has a number of wonderful prehistoric sites and Merrivale is close to the top of the list. There is a Bronze Age settlement, including a number of hut circles (between the road and the stone rows) and two double stone rows separated by a stream. The longer, southern stone row (furthest from the road) includes the remains of a cairn circle in the middle, while 50m to the south-east of this is a cist (a box-shaped burial chamber) with a split cover stone. To the south of the stone rows is a stone circle and beyond this is a large standing stone, or menhir, that is over 3m high.

WALK 4
Princetown and King's Tor

Start/finish	National Park Visitor Centre, Princetown
Locate	///october.challenge.emporium
Cafes/pubs	Choice of pubs and cafes in Princetown
Transport	Buses to Princetown from Exeter and Tavistock
Parking	Pay-and-display car park beside the National Park Visitor Centre (PL20 6QF)
Toilets	At car park

Time 3hr
Distance 11km (6¾ miles)
Climb 140m

A long, but fairly easy walk with gentle gradients, following a former railway track, passing old granite quarries and visiting King's Tor

From Princetown the walk follows the course of a former railway, before visiting Foggintor Quarry. The route then continues along the old railway, making a quick detour up to King's Tor for the view, before continuing past Swelltor Quarry. A short climb leads back to the track used on the outward route, which returns you to Princetown. The walk follows good tracks, with the exception of the loop up King's Tor, and can be shortened if required.

Sheep on the former railway after leaving Princetown

SHORT WALKS DARTMOOR — SOUTH

1 Stand facing the National Park Visitor Centre in **Princetown** (for information about Princetown see Walk 5) and turn right along the road (toilets on the left), then left along the road signed for Station Cottages. Continue past the car park (left) and immediately after passing the fire station, fork left along a path (Princetown Railway path and cycle route). Pass through a gate and continue with a fence on your right. Then keep ahead along the track for 20min, passing over a bridge to arrive at a second bridge. To the left, on a clear day, you can see the English Channel.

2 Continue along the track for 10min to a four-way junction. Turn right and follow the track for 500m, passing **Foggintor Quarry**. Ignore the first quarry entrance on the right to arrive at a second entrance on the right, with the last set of ruins on the left.

From here you can turn right to visit the flooded quarry (caution: it is rocky with deep water). The quarry, which opened in 1820 and closed in the early 20th century, provided the granite for Nelson's Column in London.

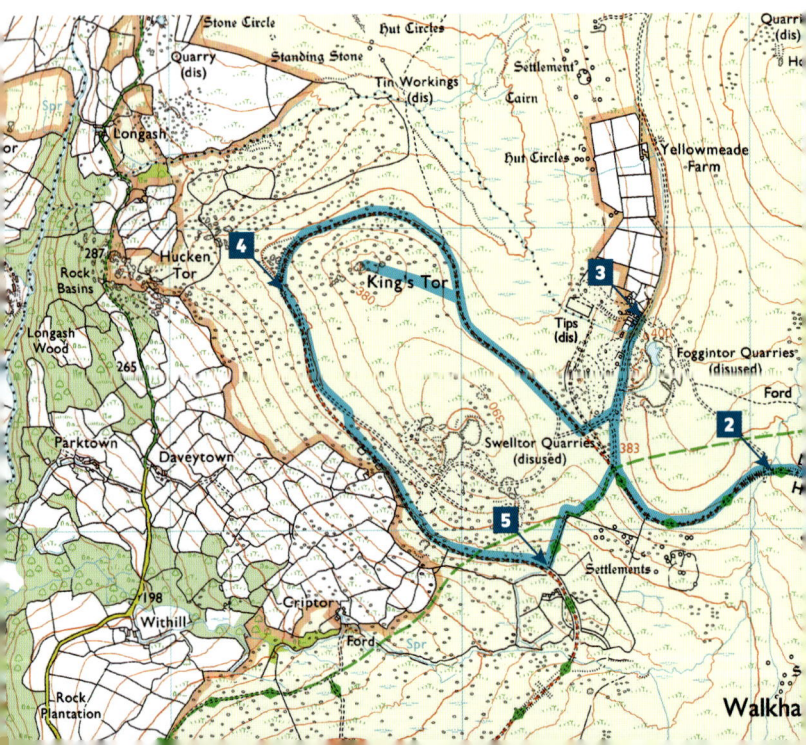

WALK 4 – PRINCETOWN AND KING'S TOR

3 Retrace your steps past the two entrances to a junction and turn right. Cross straight over a track to another track junction and turn right. Follow the fairly level track that skirts anti-clockwise round King's Tor. After 600m (10min) fork left on a path up to enjoy the views from **King's Tor** (388m) – a good picnic spot.

Look to the TV mast near Princetown (east) and move clockwise for views to Sharpitor and Ingra Tor (south), Walkham Valley to Pew Tor and Vixen Tor (west), Cox Tor and Great Staple Tor above Merrivale Quarry (north-west), and Great Mis Tor (north).

Retrace your steps back to the track and turn left. Continue along the track as it curves left, later passing through a cutting to a bridge.

4 Continue for 150m to a junction. Fork slightly left along an old siding towards **Swelltor Quarries** for 250m to some worked granite blocks on the left. These 12 abandoned corbels were made for the widening of London

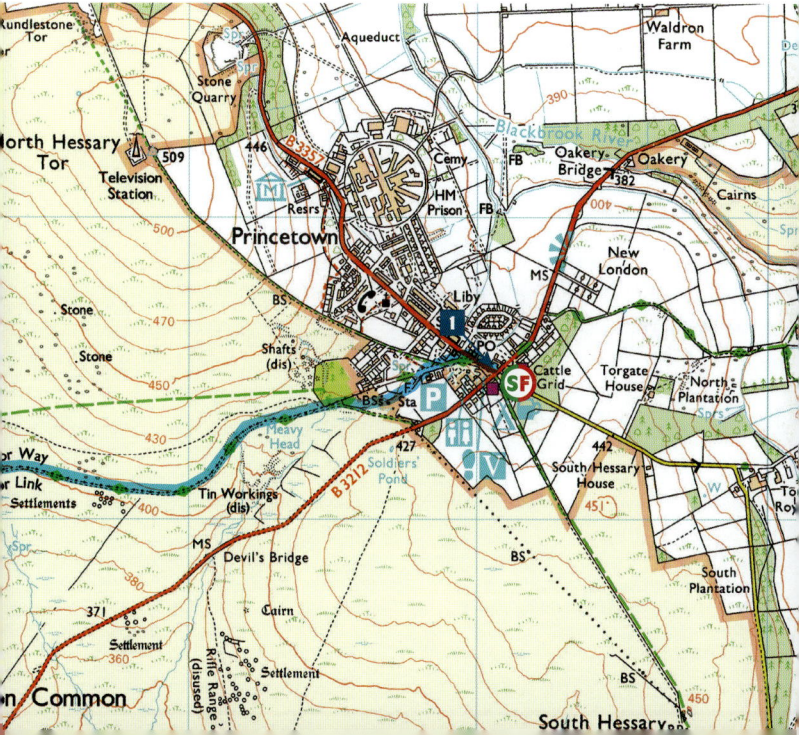

King's Tor

WALK 4 – PRINCETOWN AND KING'S TOR

Bridge in the early 1900s but were either rejected or not required. Having arrived at the corbels, fork right down across the grass to rejoin the track and bear left. Pass below the quarry spoil heaps to a wall on the left.

5 Immediately before this wall, turn left up a track with the wall on your right. At the wall corner follow the track to the right and then swing left and continue uphill to the four-way junction visited earlier. Turn right and retrace your steps along the track back to **Princetown**.

> **– To shorten**
>
> Turn around at Waypoint 3 and retrace the route back to Princetown. This shortens the walk by 4km (1hr).

Princetown Railway

The track used for most of this walk was once part of Princetown Railway, which ran from Princetown to Yelverton where it connected to the line between Plymouth and Tavistock. The branch line opened in 1883 and closed in 1956. It replaced an earlier horse-drawn tramway – the Plymouth and Dartmoor Tramway – that was built in the early 19th century for Sir Thomas Tyrwhitt to transport quarried granite down to Sutton Harbour in Plymouth.

The flooded quarry at Foggintor

Nun's (or Siward's) Cross

WALK 5
Princetown and Nun's Cross

Time 2¾hr
Distance 9.5km (6 miles)
Climb 135m

Start/finish	*National Park Visitor Centre, Princetown*
Locate	*///october.challenge.emporium*
Cafes/pubs	*Choice of pubs and cafes in Princetown*
Transport	*Buses to Princetown from Exeter and Tavistock*
Parking	*Pay-and-display car park beside the National Park Visitor Centre (PL20 6QF)*
Toilets	*At car park*

Views of an infamous Dartmoor mire, an ancient wayside cross, and an important manmade watercourse

A long, but fairly level walk with gentle gradients. From Princetown the walk follows a good track past South Hessary Tor over open moor. Then it's a narrow path alongside Devonport Leat with views over the infamous Foxtor Mires before arriving at Nun's Cross, probably the best known of Dartmoor's wayside crosses. From here the route follows a good track back to Princetown.

Dartmoor ponies and foal on the way to South Hessary Tor

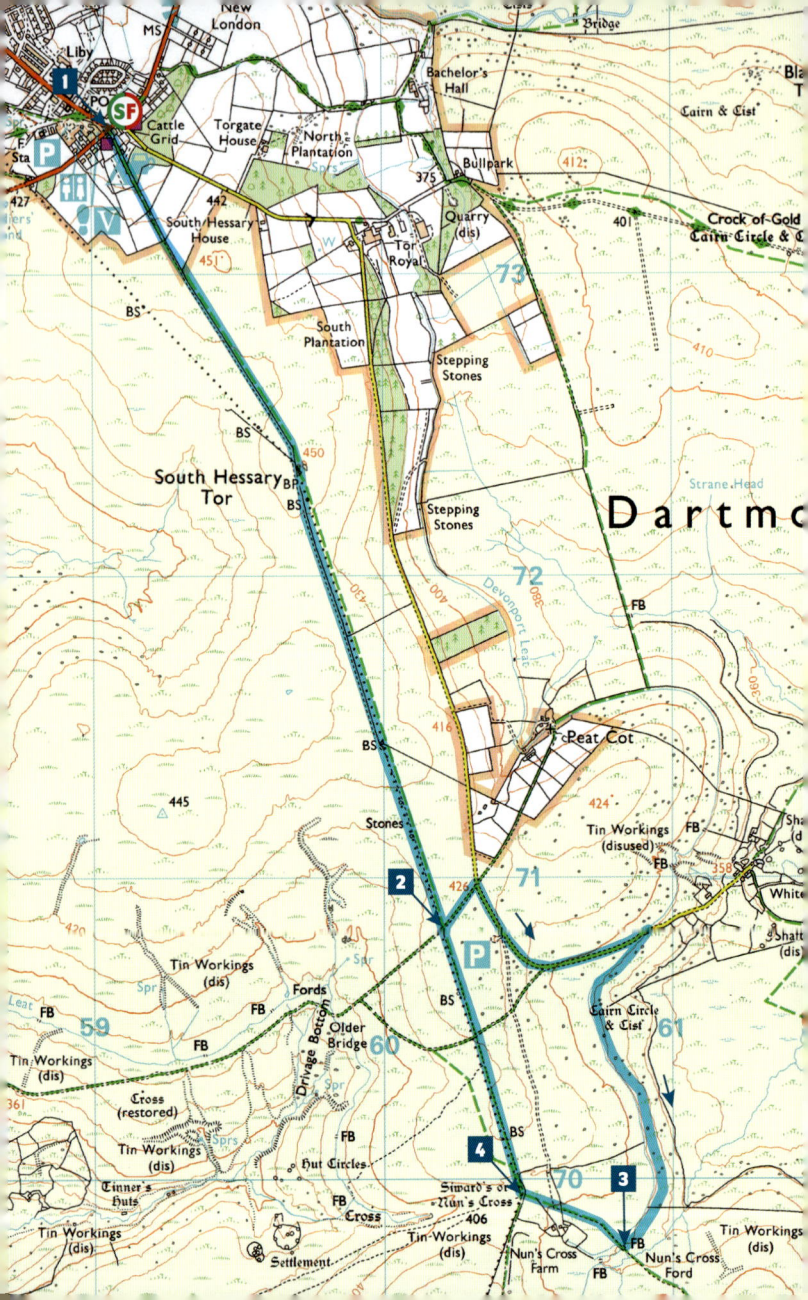

WALK 5 – PRINCETOWN AND NUN'S CROSS

1 Stand with your back to the visitor centre in **Princetown** and head over to the roundabout (junction of the B3357 and the B3212). To the left is the Fox Tor Cafe. Cross over and take the lane opposite, just left of the Plume of Feathers pub. Keep ahead along the track, go through the gate and follow the wide gravel path (bridleway) to **South Hessary Tor** (450m).

On the summit is a small cobra-shaped metal boundary marker used to mark the 1867 boundary between the Forest of Dartmoor and Walkhampton manor. The boundary stones inscribed 'PCWW 1917' seen alongside the path were erected by the Plymouth Corporation Water Works to mark the Burrator Reservoir catchment area.

Continue along the wide gravel path for just over 1.5km to a cross-track junction and boundary stone. Straight on leads directly to Nun's Cross (Waypoint 4).

2 Turn left and follow the track to a lane and parking area. Turn right along the lane, heading downhill. Immediately after crossing the bridge over the leat, turn sharp right. Follow the path alongside the Devonport Leat, which is on your right, with views to the left over Foxtor Mires.

> ⓘ *During Victorian times, Dartmoor Prison was reputed to be the harshest prison in England; visit the prison museum to find out more (www.dartmoor-prison.co.uk).*

Following the Devonport Leat with views to the left across Foxtor Mires

SHORT WALKS DARTMOOR — SOUTH

The 43km-long Devonport Leat was constructed between 1795 and 1802 to supply water to Plymouth Docks, later known as Devonport. Ignore a metal girder bridge across the leat on the way and continue to reach a clapper bridge.

The infamous Foxtor Mires are said to have been the inspiration for the fictional Grimpen Mire in Sir Arthur Conan Doyle's Sherlock Holmes novel *The Hound of the Baskervilles*. Nun's Cross Farm passed later is said to have inspired Merripit House in the same book.

3 Turn right across the bridge over the leat. Follow a grassy track that gradually bears left, keeping Nun's Cross Farm over to your left, to join a gravel track opposite **Nun's Cross**.

Known as Nun's or Siward's Cross, this is one of the oldest crosses on Dartmoor and was first mentioned in 1240 as a waymarker on the monastic route between Buckfast Abbey and Tavistock Abbey.

4 Turn right and follow the track slightly uphill to the cross-track junction visited earlier (Waypoint 2). Now keep ahead and retrace your outward route back to **Princetown**.

Nun's Cross Farmhouse (the route keeps to the right)

The former Duchy Hotel in Princetown

— To shorten

For a slightly shorter and easier walk staying on good tracks, at Waypoint 2 keep ahead along the track to Nun's Cross and then retrace the route. This reduces the walk by 2km (30min).

Princetown

Princetown is named in honour of the Prince of Wales and owes its existence to Thomas Tyrwhitt, who had a vision of creating a settlement on the high moor in the late 18th century. He established the Tor Royal Farm, built the Plymouth and Dartmoor Tramway, and erected a prison to house French and then American prisoners of war; HMP Dartmoor is still in use today. It was at the former Duchy Hotel – now the Dartmoor National Park Visitor Centre – that Sir Arthur Conan Doyle stayed and started writing his famous Sherlock Holmes story *The Hound of the Baskervilles*. The village is home to England's highest brewery.

Looking back to Nun's Cross Farmhouse (Walk 5)

Parliament Rock on Crockern Tor

WALK 6
Crockern Tor and Wistman's Wood

Start/finish	Two Bridges
Locate	///goodnight.pebble.button
Cafes/pubs	Hotel at Two Bridges
Transport	Buses to Two Bridges from Yelverton, Princetown and Tavistock
Parking	Car park on the B3357 at Two Bridges (PL20 6SW)
Toilets	No public toilets on route

Time 2hr
Distance 7km (4¼ miles)
Climb 155m

A walk with easy gradients in the West Dart Valley, visiting fascinating tors and a rare ancient woodland

From Two Bridges, home to the late 18th-century Two Bridges Hotel, follow a broad ridge heading north up the West Dart River valley, passing Crockern Tor, Littaford Tor and Longaford Tor. After exploring and admiring the views from each of the tors, drop down into the valley before heading back to Two Bridges, passing Wistman's Wood, with its ancient moss and lichen-covered trees, on the way.

Dartmoor pony at Littaford Tors

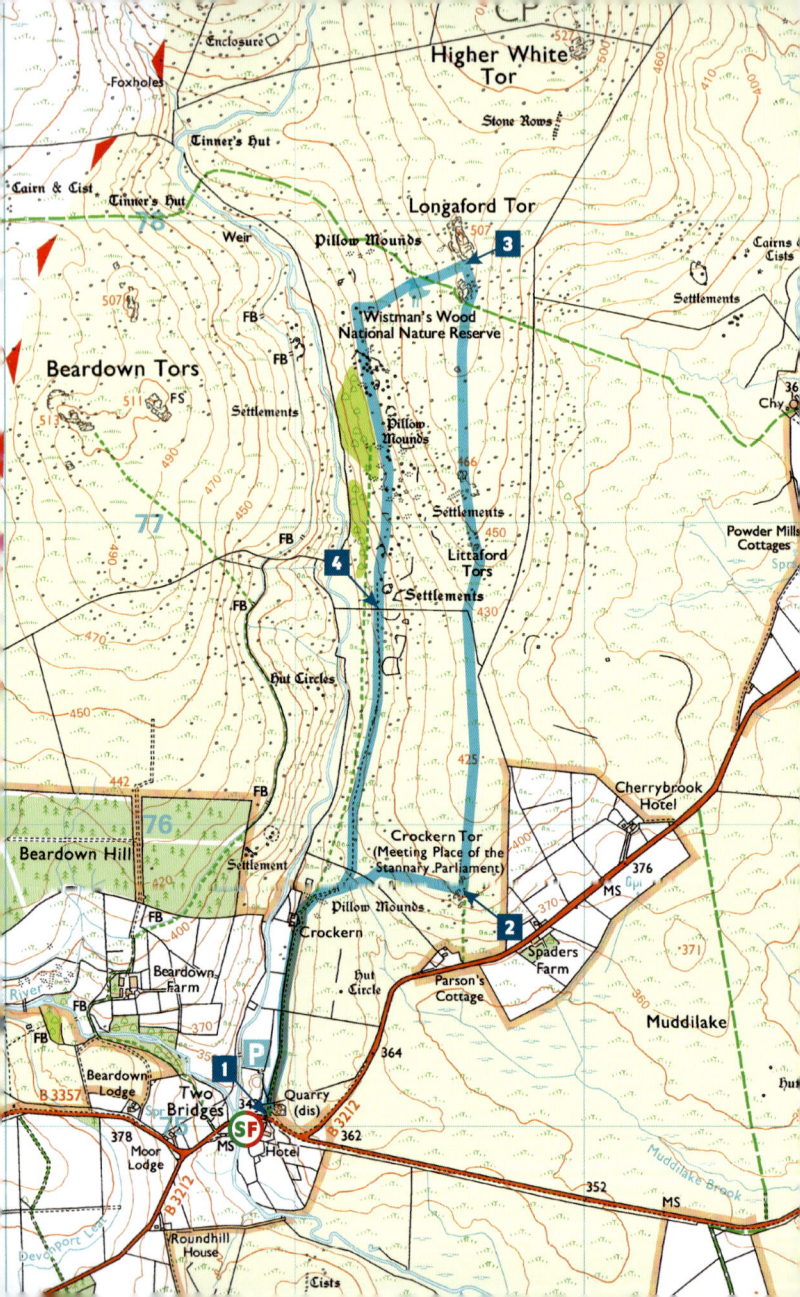

WALK 6 – CROCKERN TOR AND WISTMAN'S WOOD

1 From the B3357 at **Two Bridges** with the hotel behind you, follow the track past a small parking area (right), heading away from the hotel. Go through a gate and follow the track along the valley. Pass to the right of a house, keeping to the track as it bears right. As it bears left towards a wall and gateway, fork right on a path to reach another gap in the wall further to your right. Go through the wall gap, keep ahead for a few paces and then bear half-right on a path up towards **Crockern Tor**.

Crockern Tor and the Parliament Rock (the lower of the three outcrops) was the meeting place of the Stannary Parliament between the 14th and 18th centuries. The stannary towns – where taxes on tin were collected – were Ashburton, Chagford, Tavistock and Plympton.

2 Turn left and follow the broad ridge northwards to the top right corner of a wall. Cross the stile and continue in the same direction up to **Littaford Tors** (466m). Keep ahead along the broad ridge. Pass an outcrop at **Longaford Tor** (507m) and just before reaching the pyramid-shaped main outcrop, come to a path junction.

> ⓘ Ashburton, a former stannary town (a centre for the administration of tin-mining), is the largest town within the national park; visit the Ashburton History Museum to find out more.

The Two Bridges Hotel

Views from Longaford Tor include Beardown Tors to the west across the West Dart valley, the mast near Princetown (south-west), Bellever Tor (south-east) and Higher White Tor and Rough Tor (north).

3 Turn left and follow the path down into the valley to reach a stand of trees over to the right. Turn left and follow a path along the valley, passing above and left of **Wistman's Wood** to a wall and stile.

4 Cross over the stile and continue along the valley heading towards Two Bridges. On nearing a wall, bear slightly left and go through the wall gap. Keep ahead and retrace the outward route along the track past the house (right) back to **Two Bridges**.

− To shorten

From Waypoint 2, after crossing the stile turn left down beside the wall to a path junction (to the right is Wistman's Wood) and turn left over the stile. Now continue from Waypoint 4. This shortens the walk by 2.5km (45min).

+ To lengthen

From Longaford Tor bear half-right and follow a path up to Higher White Tor (527m), then retrace your steps to continue the route. This adds slightly under 2km (30min).

Wistman's Wood

Wistman's Wood National Nature Reserve, tucked along the West Dart Valley, is one of only three high-level ancient oak woods in Dartmoor, the others being Black-a-Tor Copse and Piles Wood. This is a rare and fragile environment where moss-covered pedunculate oak trees grow among large boulders clothed in rare mosses and lichens. The woodland is classed as temperate rainforest and is only found in areas subject to the influence of the sea, with high rainfall and humidity and a low annual variation in temperature. The Duchy of Cornwall estate, which owns this part of Dartmoor, hope to increase the size of Wistman's Wood through natural regeneration.

WALK 7
Devonport Leat and Crazy Well Pool

Time 2hr
Distance 7km (4¼ miles)
Climb 180m

Follow a picturesque leat and visit a 'bottomless' pool and a wayside cross

Start/finish	Norsworthy Bridge
Locate	///cadet.riverboat.necklaces
Cafes/pubs	None on route
Transport	No public transport
Parking	Car park at Norsworthy Bridge, Burrator Reservoir (PL20 6PF)
Toilets	No public toilets on route

From Norsworthy Bridge the route gradually climbs up through Norsworthy and Stanlake Plantations to join up with the Devonport Leat. Then you follow the leat out onto the open moor before crossing an aqueduct and heading steeply up Raddick Hill. After leaving the leat the route visits Crazy Well Pool and a wayside cross before heading down Raddick Lane on the way back to Norsworthy Bridge.

Crazy Well Pool, looking to Leather Tor and Sharpitor

SHORT WALKS DARTMOOR — SOUTH

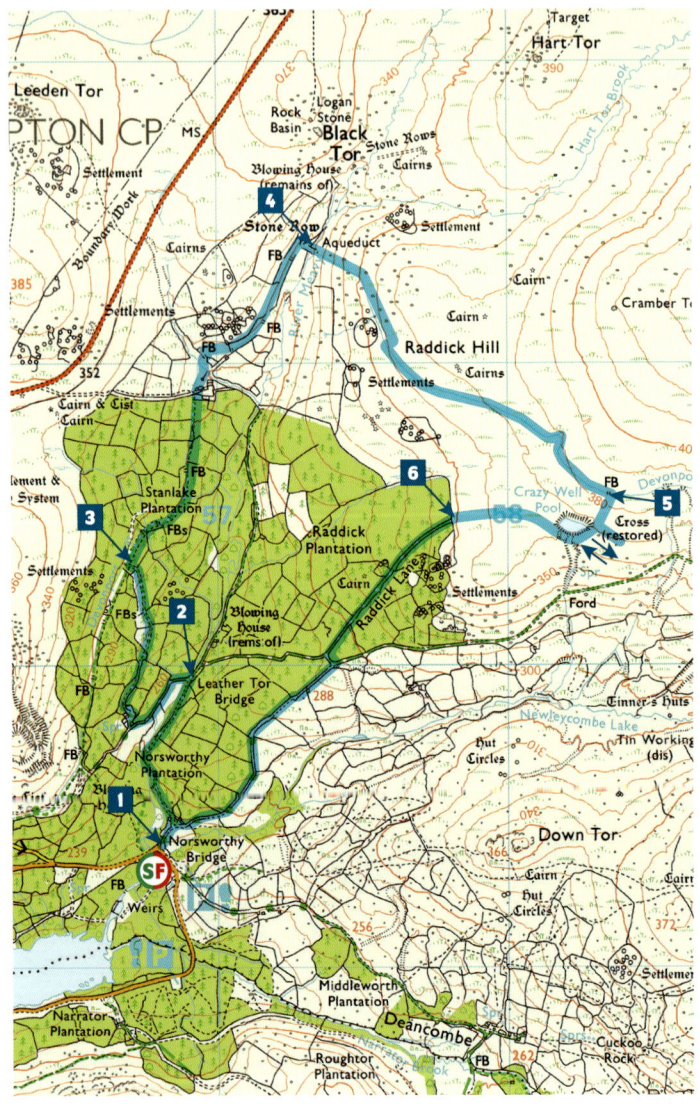

WALK 7 – DEVONPORT LEAT AND CRAZY WELL POOL

1 At the left-hand bend, just before **Norsworthy Bridge**, turn right up the track to a junction and turn left along a bridleway track. After 125m a gap in the fence on the left gives access to the tree-shaded River Meavy. Look out for the ruins of a blowing house and several mortar stones beside the river where tin ore was crushed and smelted. Continue up the track to a signed track junction.

2 Turn left (bridleway to Leathertor Farm) and cross **Leather Tor Bridge**. Follow the track as its curves to the left to reach a track junction with a gate and stile on the right. Cross the stile and follow the track past the ruins of Leathertor Farm. The farm was abandoned in the early 20th century. Continue alongside the fence on your right up to a signed path junction beside a clapper bridge over the **Devonport Leat**; on the opposite side is a granite memorial seat.

> The 43km-long Devonport Leat starts at a weir on the West Dart River north of Wistman's Wood (Walk 6). It was built in the late 18th century to supply water to Plymouth Docks (later known as Devonport).

The ruins of Leathertor Farm

Following the Devonport Leat through Stanlake Plantation

3 Do not cross the bridge but turn right (path to Stanlake Farm) and cross the stile beside the gate. Continue alongside the leat (left), through **Stanlake Plantation**. Go through a gate onto the open moor and keep ahead, following the leat, still on your left, as it soon curves to the right along a raised section. Then cross over via the clapper bridge and continue, now with the leat on your right. Later, follow the leat as it swings right to reach an aqueduct over the **River Meavy**.

4 Go through gates at either end of the **aqueduct** and continue steeply uphill, keeping the leat on your right as it tumbles down the hill. On reaching a clapper bridge, cross over and continue skirting round **Raddick Hill** with the leat on your left. Later the leat makes a sharp horseshoe shaped curve and passes a sluice gate before continuing to a clapper bridge on your left.

5 Turn right downhill, heading away from the leat, to a path junction at the lower edge of **Crazy Well Pool**. The onward route turns right, but before that turn left for 75m to visit a stone cross, then retrace your steps.

WALK 7 – DEVONPORT LEAT AND CRAZY WELL POOL

Crazy Well Pool, once thought to be bottomless but actually less than 5m deep, is the result of tin mining in the area. Crazy Well Cross nearby is a medieval wayside marker on the monastic route between Tavistock and Buckfast.

Follow the path alongside the lower edge of the pool, with the water on your right, to a three-way path junction. Take the middle option straight on towards the trees, with Sharpitor on the skyline, to reach the edge of **Raddick Plantation**.

6 Go through the gate and follow the enclosed track (**Raddick Lane**) down through Raddick Plantation to a track junction. Turn left for a few paces to another junction and turn right down the track, with trees on your right. On reaching the track junction passed earlier, keep left back down to **Norsworthy Bridge**.

> **+ To lengthen**
>
> At the sharp right bend just before the aqueduct at Waypoint 4, fork left (straight on) along a path with an old wall on your left and continue up the valley to a tree and a small waterfall, beside the ruins of a blowing house – a great picnic spot. Retrace your steps and turn left to continue the route. This adds 600m (15min).

Crazy Well Cross, looking to Burrator Reservoir

Church and cross in Sheepstor

WALK 8
Meavy and Sheepstor

Start/finish	*Meavy village green*
Locate	*///adapt.entrusted.madder*
Cafes/pubs	*Pub at Meavy*
Transport	*Buses to Meavy from Tavistock and Yelverton*
Parking	*On street in Meavy, or at reservoir (PL20 6PJ)*
Toilets	*At Burrator Reservoir*

Time 2½hr
Distance 7.5km (4¾ miles)
Climb 280m

Two picturesque villages, a peaceful reservoir and a tor with a view

From the peaceful village of Meavy, the walk heads through woods to Burrator Reservoir, built in 1898 to supply water to Plymouth. After leaving the reservoir it's a bit of a climb up to Sheeps Tor for a great view, before heading down to Sheepstor village. Then it's off along lanes and tracks back to Meavy, passing the Marchant's Cross on the way. The walk may also be started from Waypoint 2.

View over Burrator Reservoir from Sheeps Tor

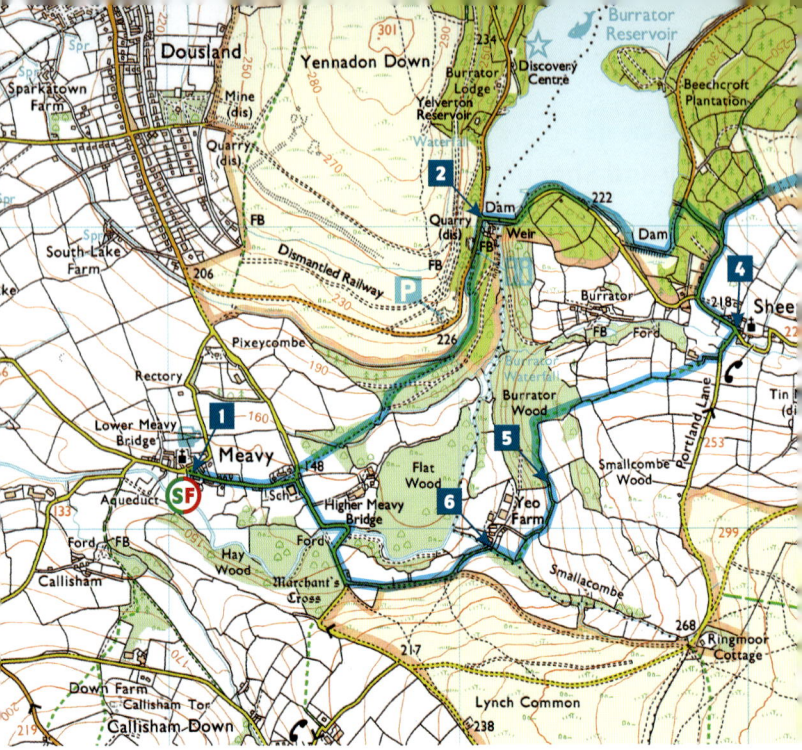

1 With your back to the parish hall, stand facing the village green and pub in **Meavy** and turn right along the road to a junction beside the primary school. Overlooking the village green is an ancient oak tree, the village cross, the 500-year-old Royal Oak pub and the 15th-century St Peter's Church. Turn left in the direction of Dousland for a few metres, then turn right through a gate (footpath sign). Cross the field, then continue through the trees and two gates to enter a wood. Fork left following a path up to Drake's (or Plymouth) Leat. The leat was built in the 16th century to supply water to Plymouth. Bear right alongside the former leat to a track and footpath sign. Turn left up the track, pass a gate and bear right along the road, passing the toilets, to a junction at **Burrator Reservoir**.

2 Turn right, crossing the dam, and continue along the road for 130m. Turn left through a gate, down some steps and turn right along the reservoir path with the water on your left. Later,

WALK 8 – MEAVY AND SHEEPSTOR

cross a smaller **dam** and follow the path as it swings left. Leave through a gate and turn right along the lane to a right-hand bend and bridleway junction. Turn left up the enclosed bridleway. Keep right along the lane for the shortcut. Go through a gate onto the open moor and keep ahead up to the top of **Sheeps Tor**.

3 After soaking up the view over Burrator Reservoir, turn around and retrace your steps back down to the lane. Keep left to a T-junction and turn left to a junction in **Sheepstor**, beside a stone cross (left) with the church beyond.

> The 15th-century St Leonard's Church houses a fine wooden rood screen and carved oak bench-ends. In the churchyard are

Seat by Burrator Reservoir

the tombs of three members of the Brooke family, who, between them, ruled as Rajahs of Sarawak (now part of Malaysia) from 1841 until 1946.

4 Turn right along the lane for 100m, then turn right through a gate (footpath sign). Follow the track towards a house and bear half-left into a field. Continue up to the top right corner and go through a small gate adjacent to the field gate. Follow the right-hand field edge, passing some large boulders. At the corner go over the stone step stile and follow the enclosed path, crossing another stile. Dogleg right and bear left through **Burrator Wood**, following the boundary on your left as it swings left. Continue to the boundary corner beside a large tree.

5 Turn left over the boundary, down a ladder stile and turn right along the enclosed route to a track. Bear right and just before the track heads more steeply downhill, fork left. Cross a stile beside a gate and follow the enclosed path downhill. Cross another stile and follow a fence on your right as it swings right (stream on the left). Then cross stiles either side of a footbridge to join a lane opposite **Yeo House** (Yeo Farm).

6 Turn left along the lane to a junction beside the **Marchant's Cross**. This 13th-century wayside cross is inscribed with a simple Latin cross symbol. Turn right down the road, following it across the River Meavy to a three-way junction and turn left (in the direction of Yelverton) back to the village green in **Meavy**.

The Royal Oak pub at Meavy

The Marchant's Cross

− To shorten

Miss out the section up to Sheeps Tor by continuing along the lane instead of turning up the bridleway. This reduces the walk by 1.5km (45min) and saves 120m climbing.

ⓘ *In the gable of the primary school roof in Meavy is a replica of the drum that Sir Francis Drake took with him when he circumnavigated the world. The drum was used to summon pupils to school.*

The ford across the Drizzle Combe stream on the way to the stone rows (Walk 9)

Following the track towards Ditsworthy Warren House

WALK 9
Ditsworthy and Drizzlecombe

Start/finish	*Gutter Tor car park*
Locate	*///should.luckier.salt*
Cafes/pubs	*None on route*
Transport	*No public transport*
Parking	*Gutter Tor car park (PL20 6PG)*
Toilets	*No public toilets on route*

Time 2hr
Distance 6.5km (4 miles)
Climb 150m

Visit a film location, an impressive prehistoric site and the ruins of an old tin mine

From Gutter Tor car park this walk follows a reasonably level track to Ditsworthy Warren House. Then the terrain gets a bit more interesting with a stream to splodge across before heading gradually up to the impressive Bronze Age relics at Drizzlecombe. The route follows a path up to Hartor Tor – a good place to sit and admire the views – before heading over to the ruins of Eylesbarrow Tin Mine. The final section follows a good track back down to the car park.

View from Higher Hartor Tor

1 At the car park stand facing towards Gutter Tor and walk up the grassy slope, heading away from the road to join a gravel track beside a gate. Turn left along this for just over 1km to arrive at **Ditsworthy Warren House**.

> The 18th-century Ditsworthy Warren House (private) was used by the keeper of the Ditsworthy Warren, which was used to farm rabbits until it was abandoned in the 1940s. Avid film watchers might recognise the house, as it was used in Steven Spielberg's film *War Horse* (2010).

2 Pass to the left of the building and follow the track along the valley for 600m, with the River Plym some distance over to the right. Now it gets a bit challenging as there is a shallow stream to cross via a ford and some stones. There's no footbridge, so if the stream is flooded turn back and save the walk for a drier day. Once

WALK 9 – DITSWORTHY AND DRIZZLECOMBE

across, continue up the path to a large standing stone at the start of the first **stone row** at Drizzlecombe.

3 Continue up beside the stones, passing the **Giant's Basin** over to the right. Pass the 'Bone Stone' and continue up alongside the next stone row, then keep ahead, following a path up to **Higher Hartor Tor**. Views from here include Plymouth Sound, Sheeps Tor (west), and the distinctive outline of Brent Tor and its church (north-west). From the tor head diagonally left on a grassy path over flat ground to join a track. Turn left along this to a track junction beside the ruins of the **Eylesbarrow Tin Mine**.

The site dates from the early 19th century, and included water-powered lifting wheels, a smelting house and a number of vertical shafts and adits (horizontal shafts), which were cut to reach the tin lodes.

4 Follow the track downhill. Later keep right at a split junction and near the bottom pass a stand of trees surrounding a building on the left to reach the **car park**.

One of the stone rows at Drizzlecombe

Dartmoor ponies beside the ruins of Eylesbarrow Tin Mine

— To shorten

For a much shorter and easier walk, head to Ditsworthy Warren House (Waypoint 2) and then retrace your steps. This reduces the walk by 4km (1hr).

ⓘ *A large part of Dartmoor is made of granite created around 295 million years ago. Subsequent weathering and erosion have formed the characteristic tors that can be seen today.*

Drizzlecombe

Drizzlecombe, located on a spur of land between the River Plym on the right and Drizzle Combe on the left, is home to an impressive collection of Bronze Age relics. The most visible are the three stone rows, which incorporate two very large standing stones, including the 4.2m-high 'Bone Stone'. There is also a large burial cairn, 22m in diameter, known as the Giant's Basin. Further up the slope, beyond the stone rows, are the remains of ancient enclosed settlements and hut circles. Dotted around the area are more stone cairns and cists or kistvaens – box-shaped stone coffins.

WALK 10
Ivybridge and Henlake Down

Time 1½hr
Distance 5km (3 miles)
Climb 160m

A low-level woodland walk beside the River Erme and then a loop over open heathland

Start/finish	The Watermark, Ivybridge
Locate	///nail.realm.weeps
Cafes/pubs	Choice of pubs and cafes in Ivybridge
Transport	Trains to Ivybridge station (1.3km from start). Buses from Plymouth, Paignton and Exeter stop at the town hall (100m from start)
Parking	Leonards Road car park (PL21 0SZ), or on street
Toilets	Ivybridge

From The Watermark, a combined arts venue, library and cafe, the walk follows a short section of the Two Moors Way. Then it's off along the Dartmoor Way following the River Erme upstream, passing under an impressive viaduct on the way. You then leave the river behind to climb Henlake Down for some views before heading back down to Ivybridge. Some of the paths may be muddy after wet weather.

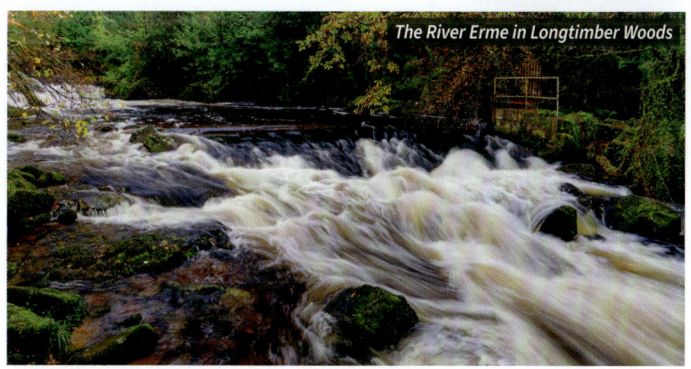
The River Erme in Longtimber Woods

SHORT WALKS DARTMOOR — SOUTH

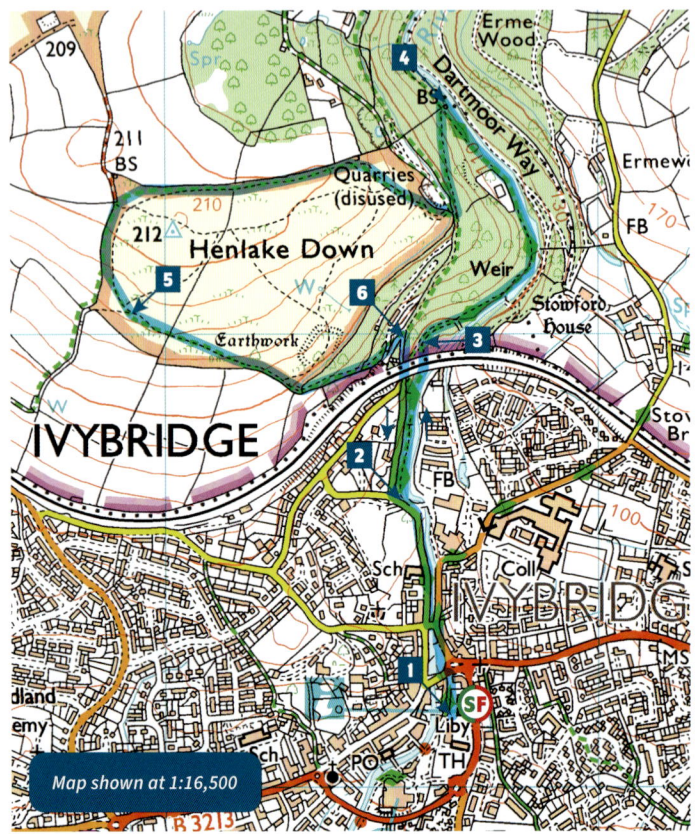

Map shown at 1:16,500

1 Stand facing The Watermark in **Ivybridge**, turn left, then right along Costly Street to a T-junction. Turn left for a few paces and then right across the road to follow the signed Two Moors Way path through the car park, with the River Erme on the left. Spot the old electricity generating turbine, known locally as 'the Snail' due to its shape. Then bear right and continue along Harford Road for a few metres to a junction and turn left over the Ivy Bridge to a cross-junction. Turn right along Station Road, now following the Dartmoor Way, to reach the entrance to the former Stowford Mill (right).

WALK 10 – IVYBRIDGE AND HENLAKE DOWN

2 Keep ahead along the signed path through the trees, with the **River Erme** on your right and road up to the left. Cross a footbridge and continue, passing under the viaduct to a junction with a track.

> The first viaduct was built for Isambard Kingdom Brunel's broad-gauge railway in 1848. Only the piers survive. It was replaced in 1894 with the current viaduct, built to carry two standard-gauge tracks.

3 Bear right along the track through Longtimber Wood, keeping the river on your right, later passing an old stone wall on the left. Originally a sheep pound, this site was later used as a small reservoir and then a swimming pool in the 1920s, but this closed in the 1960s. Continue to a signed three-way junction.

4 Turn sharp left up to a lane. Turn right for a few paces, then turn left through a gate. Keep right uphill and later the path swings left to follow a wall on the right. Just before the top right corner, turn left down the wide path following the right-hand side of **Henlake Down**, with views over Ivybridge to the coast.

5 Keep left at a path junction, heading downhill, and go through a gate. Follow the enclosed path downhill, passing under a small bridge to join a lane.

An old water turbine nicknamed 'The Snail'

SHORT WALKS DARTMOOR — SOUTH

On Henlake Down heading back towards Ivybridge

6 Turn right and follow the lane downhill. Pass under the **viaduct** and keep left (straight on) at the junction down Station Road to Waypoint 2. Then retrace your steps back to The Watermark. Alternatively, on reaching the cross-junction beside the Ivy Bridge, keep ahead along Erme Road to the War Memorial. Turn left across the bridge then turn right along Costly Street back to The Watermark.

> **– To shorten**
>
> At Waypoint 4 turn sharp left up to the lane and then turn left down to Waypoint 6. This reduces the walk by 1.5km (30min).

Ivybridge

The town is named after the 'Ivybrugge', an Ivy-covered packhorse bridge built across the River Erme. First mentioned in 1292, the bridge was widened in the 18th century to allow horse-drawn stagecoaches to cross on their way between Exeter and Plymouth. In 1813 the bridge was the subject of a painting by JMW Turner. The fast-flowing River Erme, which rises high up on the moors, was used to power a number of mills in the town for milling corn, fulling cloth and making paper.

The viaduct at Ivybridge

Hangershell Rock makes a good picnic spot

WALK 11

Butterdon Hill and Western Beacon

Start/finish	Ivybridge railway station
Locate	///wobbling.fault.spice
Cafes/pubs	Plenty of choice in Ivybridge (800m off route)
Transport	Trains to Ivybrige. Buses from Plymouth, Paignton and Exeter stop on the B3213 (500m from start)
Parking	Station car park (PL21 0DQ), or roadside parking in Cole Lane
Toilets	Ivybridge town centre (1km off route)

Time 3hr
Distance 9.5km (6 miles)
Climb 280m

Follow the Two Moors Way along a former tramway, pass some prehistoric remains and visit Dartmoor's most southerly summit

From Ivybridge railway station the walk soon leaves the town, following the Two Moors Way to climb onto the open moor. A former tramway track takes you past Hangershell Rock before heading south, following the remains of an ancient stone row up to Butterdon Hill. After a short descent to pass the Black Pool the route arrives at Western Beacon – Dartmoor's most southerly top. From here it's downhill back towards Ivybridge before you retrace your steps back to the start.

The track towards the open moor

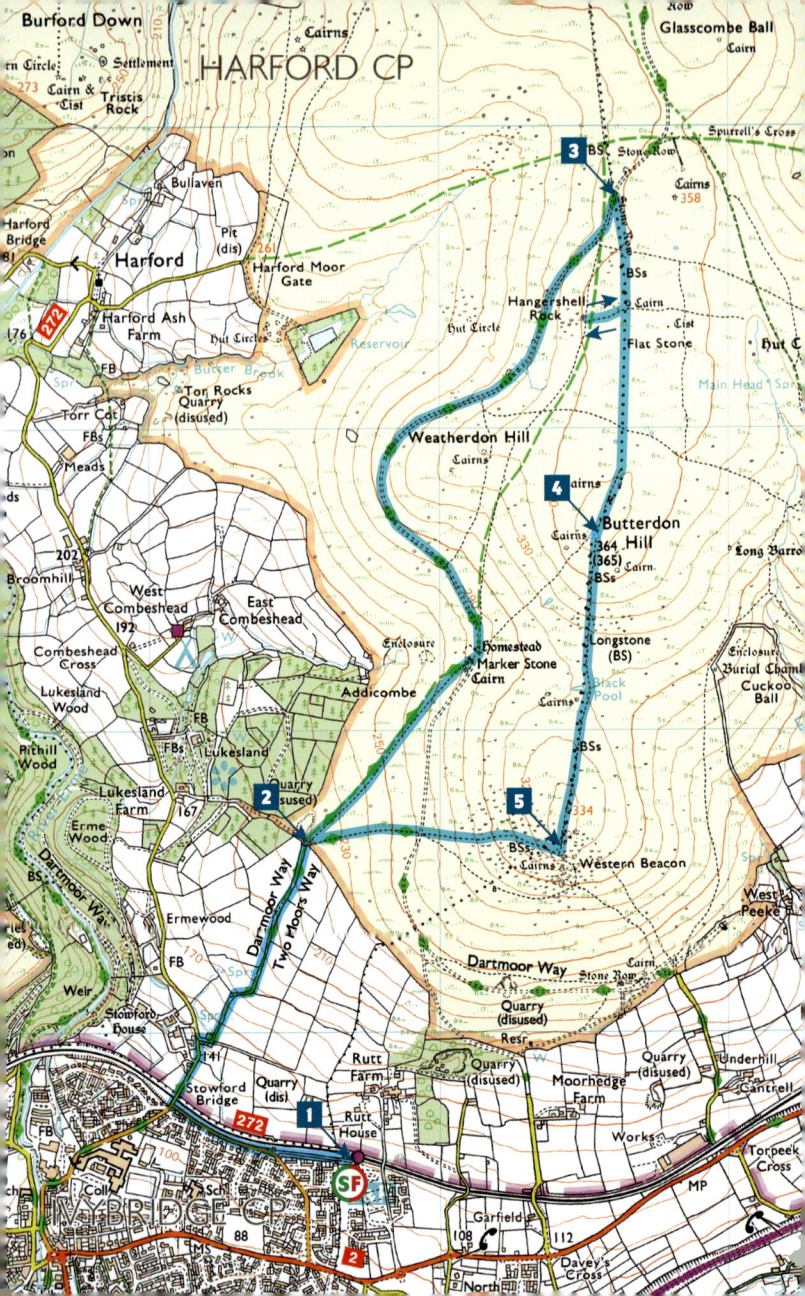

WALK 11 – BUTTERDON HILL AND WESTERN BEACON

1 With the **railway station** behind you (car park ahead), turn right along the combined footpath and cycleway. Pass the bus stop and continue along Cole Lane to a road junction on the right. Turn right (in the direction of Harford/Lukesland). The road to the left leads down to the centre of Ivybridge (800m each way with the toilets a further 200m). Cross **Stowford Bridge** over the railway and continue up the lane to Stowford Farm (left). Turn right along an enclosed track with a bridleway signpost for 800m, following the Two Moors Way and Dartmoor Way up to a gate.

2 Go through the gate onto the open moor where the route splits. Keep ahead up the wide grassy bridleway (Two Moors Way), with trees and a wall some distance over to the left. On reaching a track beside a Two Moors Way **marker stone**, turn left.

The track was originally the route of the 13km-long narrow-gauge tramway – known locally as the 'Puffing Billy' – built in 1911 to transport supplies and workers between Bittaford and the Red Lake china clay works.

Follow the track for 2km (30min), skirting round **Weatherdon Hill**. The route passes below the distinctive Hangershell Rock on your right and later reaches a crossing stone row.

Dating from the Late Neolithic or early Bronze Age, Butterdon Hill Stone Row is the second longest stone row on Dartmoor. It consists of a line of fairly small stones, partly hidden in the vegetation, running on a north–south alignment for 2km between Piles Hill and Butterdon Hill.

3 Turn sharp right here and follow a path up beside the stone row to the remains of a burial cairn (5min). Turn right for 150m to visit **Hangershell Rock** – a great picnic spot – then retrace your steps and turn right. Continue southwards along the course of the stone row to the trig point on **Butterdon Hill** (364m), passing two Bronze Age stone burial cairns on the way. There are views ahead of Western Beacon, to the right is Plymouth, to the left is Ugborough Beacon and behind you are Stalldown Barrow, Sharp Tor and Three Barrows (left to right).

4 Continue straight on down to a saddle, following a line of boundary stones which includes the Longstone, a taller than average boundary stone. Keep ahead, passing the **Black Pool** (this may be dry in summer) and head

The former tramway past Hangershell Rock

uphill. Pass just to the right of a stone burial cairn before reaching a pair of stone burial cairns and a small boundary stone on **Western Beacon** (334m). From the summit there is another great view over the South Hams to the sea.

5 On reaching the pair of burial cairns, turn right (west) and head downhill. Cross straight over the track (a continuation of the former tramway used earlier) and continue down the wide grassy path to the gate passed earlier (Waypoint 2). Go through the gate and retrace your outward route back to the start.

> **– To shorten**
>
> On reaching the tramway track in Waypoint 2, cross straight over and follow a path up to the trig point on Butterdon Hill. Then turn sharp right and continue the walk from Waypoint 4. This shortens the walk by 2km (45min).

> *ⓘ The Two Moors Way, a 188km long-distance coast-to-coast route from Lynmouth to Wembury (in South Devon), meanders through Dartmoor.*

WALK 12
South Brent and Shipley Bridge

Time 3¼hr
Distance 9.5km (6 miles)
Climb 315m

A challenging route with a mix of quiet lanes, woodland, rivers and open moorland

Start/finish	Station Road, South Brent
Locate	///crossword.retiring.rips
Cafes/pubs	Pub and cafe in South Brent
Transport	Buses from Paignton, Plymouth and Ivybridge stop on the B3372 in South Brent (400m off route)
Parking	Car park off Station Road (TQ10 9AL)
Toilets	South Brent and Shipley Bridge

From South Brent follow the River Avon to Lydia Bridge before joining the Dartmoor Way up over Aish Ridge to Ball Gate. After a section of open moor, it's off down Diamond Lane and on to Shipley Bridge. The return route follows the valley through Didworthy and Lutton to Lydia Bridge before you retrace your steps back to South Brent. Paths may be wet, and Diamond Lane is stony and can be slippery.

View from Aish Ridge looking north to Brent Moor

SHORT WALKS DARTMOOR — SOUTH

1 At the car park, with your back to the railway, turn left and walk up to the junction with Station Road. Turn right down to a crossroads. Fore Street (left) leads to the B3372 and bus stops, straight across are the toilets. Turn right along Church Street, passing the Toll House then Wellington Square to reach St Petroc's Church (left). Immediately after passing the church, fork left down a track (footpath to Lydia Bridge). Pass under the railway bridge, go through a gate and follow the riverside path to a lane at **Lydia Bridge**.

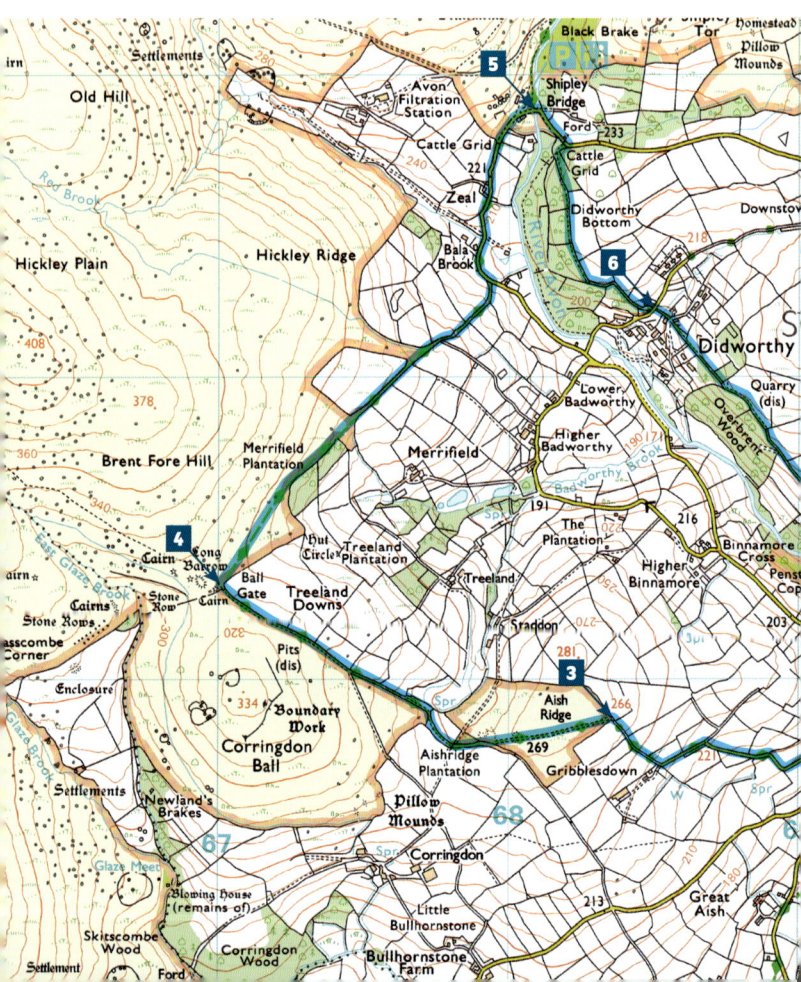

WALK 12 – SOUTH BRENT AND SHIPLEY BRIDGE

St Petroc's Church, South Brent

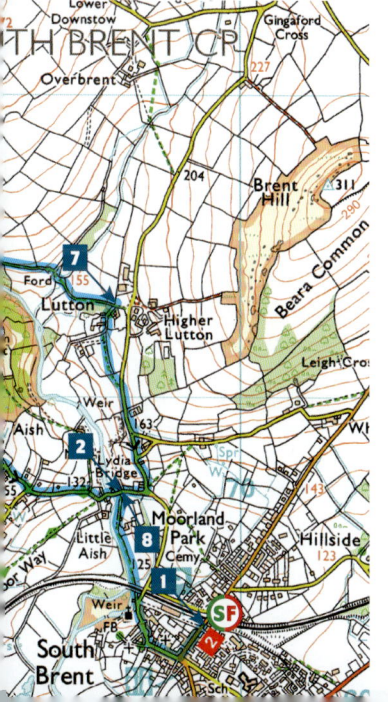

South Brent used to hold sheep fairs and markets and there is a list of market toll charges on the Toll House. Wellington Square has a Jubilee Stone with sundial, dedicated to Queen Victoria and Queen Elizabeth II. Parts of St Petroc's Church date from Saxon times and the tower is Norman.

2 Turn left across Lydia Bridge over the River Avon and follow the road uphill. The walk now follows the Dartmoor Way to Shipley Bridge. At the junction keep right up to another junction. Turn left and follow the lane up to its end at **Gribblesdown**. Turn right up the enclosed track (bridleway) and through a gate at the top.

Ball Gate leads to the open moor

3 Bear left, following a grassy track over **Aish Ridge**. There are views ahead including Ugborough Beacon, South Hams (left) and behind to Brent Hill. Follow the track down past Aishridge Plantation. Go through a gate and head uphill, passing through two gates, and then go through **Ball Gate** onto the open moor.

> The large gateposts at Ball Gate, which look slightly out of place, are from the former Brent Manor. Several large boulders 70m to the left are all that remains of a Neolithic long barrow (burial mound).

4 Turn right (bridleway to Shipley Bridge via Diamond Lane), following the Dartmoor Way over the open moor, later with a stone wall and **Merrifield Plantation** on the right. Keep ahead between walls. Then step across a stream, head downhill and go through a gate. Continue down the tree-shaded bridleway (Diamond Lane). Go through a gate and turn left along the lane to **Shipley Bridge** and the River Avon (car park, picnic tables and toilets).

5 Continue along the lane, cross a cattle grid, and as the lane bears left, turn right through a gate (footpath to Lutton and Didworthy). Cross a stile

WALK 12 – SOUTH BRENT AND SHIPLEY BRIDGE

and continue up through woodland. Later head down a concrete track past buildings to a lane at **Didworthy**.

6 Cross straight over towards the houses. Keep right at the first split, then immediately left at the next. At the private entrance (Pinewood Lodge), fork left along a narrower bridleway alongside **Overbent Wood**. Pass through two gates, heading downhill – this later becomes a track. Keep ahead through another gate, cross the stream via a footbridge and go up to a lane at **Lutton** (beside Lower Lutton Farm).

7 Turn right, then keep left with a wall on the right and pass some cottages. Go through the gate, follow the enclosed path, cross a stile and head diagonally left across the field. Cross the stile beside the field gate and turn right down the lane. Keep ahead at two junctions to a third junction (Oakhill Cross).

8 Turn right and just before **Lydia Bridge**, turn left over the stone stile and retrace the route back towards **South Brent** and from there to Station Road and the car park. Alternatively, on reaching the road near the church, turn sharp left to a junction and turn right along the lane to the car park.

> **– To shorten**
>
> Follow the route to Aish Ridge (Waypoint 3) for the view and then head back. This reduces the walk by 4.5km (1hr 15min) and saves 140m climbing.

Following the path beside Overbrent Wood

The memorial cross on the way up Corndon Tor, looking towards Yar Tor

WALK 13
Dartmeet tors

Start/finish	Dartmeet
Locate	///eyepieces.cheesy.quitter
Cafes/pubs	Cafe at the car park
Transport	Buses to Dartmeet from Tavistock and Newton Abbot (summer only)
Parking	Pay-and-display car park at Dartmeet (PL20 6SG)
Toilets	At car park

Time 2hr
Distance 5.5km (3½ miles)
Climb 265m

Follow a hilly walk from the picturesque River Dart, visiting three tors with some lovely views

From Dartmeet the route follows the Dartmoor Way up past the Coffin Stone before heading downhill to cross a stream and then up to Sharp Tor. The walking becomes easier as you head up Corndon Tor, passing a memorial cross on the way. After visiting Yar Tor there's a short, but rather steep, descent back to Dartmeet. A shorter walk with less climbing is also possible.

Looking north-east from Sharp Tor to the distant Haytor Rocks

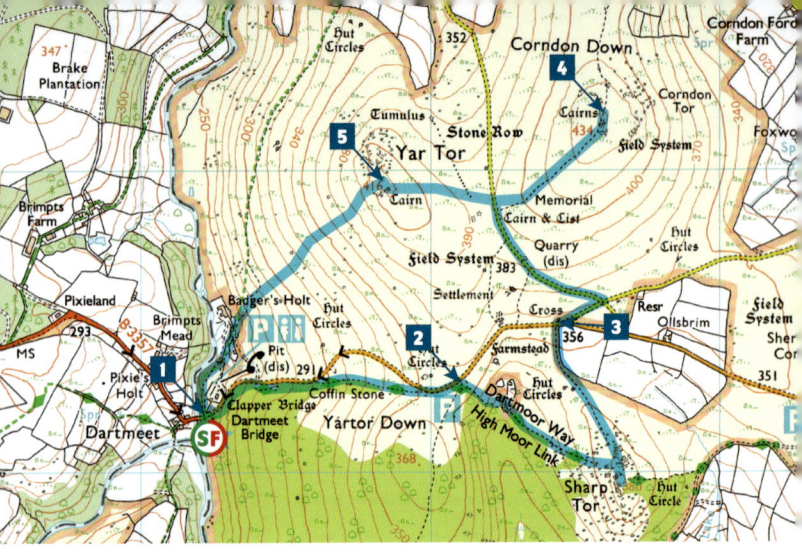

1 Start the walk at the road bridge in **Dartmeet**, with the car park and cafe behind you.

> **Dartmeet is where the East Dart and West Dart rivers meet to form the River Dart. Just upstream of the late 18th-century road bridge are the remains of an older medieval clapper bridge.**

Turn left along the road past the cattle grid and immediately fork right on a narrow path (with a Dartmoor Way High Moor Link waymark on the gate). Bear left after a few metres, following the path up through the gorse and keeping the road on your left. The path becomes more defined as it passes the **Coffin Stone**. This large boulder split in two is where the bearers would rest the coffin on the way to Widecombe in the Moor. Keep ahead up to the **car park** at the top of the rise (for the shorter walk turn left across the road).

2 Turn right and head steeply downhill. Cross the stream in the valley. (There's no footbridge and it can be boggy in winter; to avoid this section follow the road to Waypoint 3.) Keep ahead up towards **Sharp Tor** (308m). On reaching the left-hand outcrop the onward route turns left, but before that it's worth visiting the main tor.

> **Sharp Tor offers a great view. Look south over the wooded Dart Valley to Bench Tor: moving right you have Venford Reservoir, then Ryder's Hill and the mast near**

WALK 13 – DARTMEET TORS

Princetown (west), Yar Tor and Corndon Tor (north), and further round is Rippon Tor and Buckland Beacon (east).

Follow a path slightly downhill aiming between Yar Tor (left) and Corndon Tor (right). At a path junction keep right, with the wall on the right to a road junction.

3 Cross over and take the minor road opposite (signed for Sherrill and Babeny), passing the remains of a **cross**. Unfortunately, the medieval wayside cross, known as Ollsbrim or Ouldsbroom Cross, had its arms removed when it was used as a gatepost. At the next junction turn left up the lane (signed for Sherrill and Babeny) for 500m to a small parking area on the left. Turn right and follow the path uphill, soon passing a **memorial** cross. Continue up to **Corndon Tor** (434m).

Fine views from Condor Tor include Yar Tor, Hamel Down, Haytor Rocks and back to Sharp Tor. Just to the north of the summit is a large Bronze Age burial cairn.

4 Turn around and retrace the route back down to the lane. Cross straight over and follow the path up to the summit of **Yar Tor** (416m). On the summit, the remains of a Bronze Age burial cairn have been modified to form a spiral-shaped stone shelter.

The remains of the medieval clapper bridge at Dartmeet

SHORT WALKS DARTMOOR — SOUTH

5 Bear half-left down a narrow path towards Dartmeet. It's a bit steep, so take your time. At the bottom of the slope, beside a stone wall, turn left. Then keep right at the split. Go through a gate and cross the footbridge to enter the car park. Bear right over to the East Dart River and follow the path downstream past the ruins of the medieval clapper bridge back to the main road at **Dartmeet**.

> ⓘ *The hamlet of Huccaby near Dartmeet is home to the small but interesting 19th-century St Raphael's Church, which was used as a combined chapel and schoolroom. The pews are the original school desks.*

– To shorten

From the car park at Waypoint 2 turn left across the road and follow the obvious path up to Yar Tor (Waypoint 5). This reduces the walk by 2.5km (50min) and saves 95m climbing.

The spiral stone shelter on the top of Yar Tor

WALK 14
Holne and Leigh Tor

Time 2¾hr
Distance 8.5km (5¼ miles)
Climb 320m

A rather hilly walk featuring a picturesque village, riverside paths, woodland and open heath

Start/finish	Holne village hall
Locate	///gear.rate.trackers
Cafes/pubs	Pub and community shop/tea room in Holne
Transport	No public transport
Parking	On roadside and at village hall (small charge, TQ13 7SL)
Toilets	At car park at New Bridge

From Holne the walk follows the Two Moors Way to New Bridge and then alongside the picturesque River Dart through Deeper Marsh. A stiff climb takes you up to pass Leigh Tor and Aish Tor, stopping to admire the views on the way. After briefly following Dr Blackall's Drive, the route follows the Dartmoor Way down through the Dart Valley Nature Reserve to New Bridge before retracing the outward route with a steep climb back up to Holne.

Leigh Tor, looking to Buckland Beacon

SHORT WALKS DARTMOOR — SOUTH

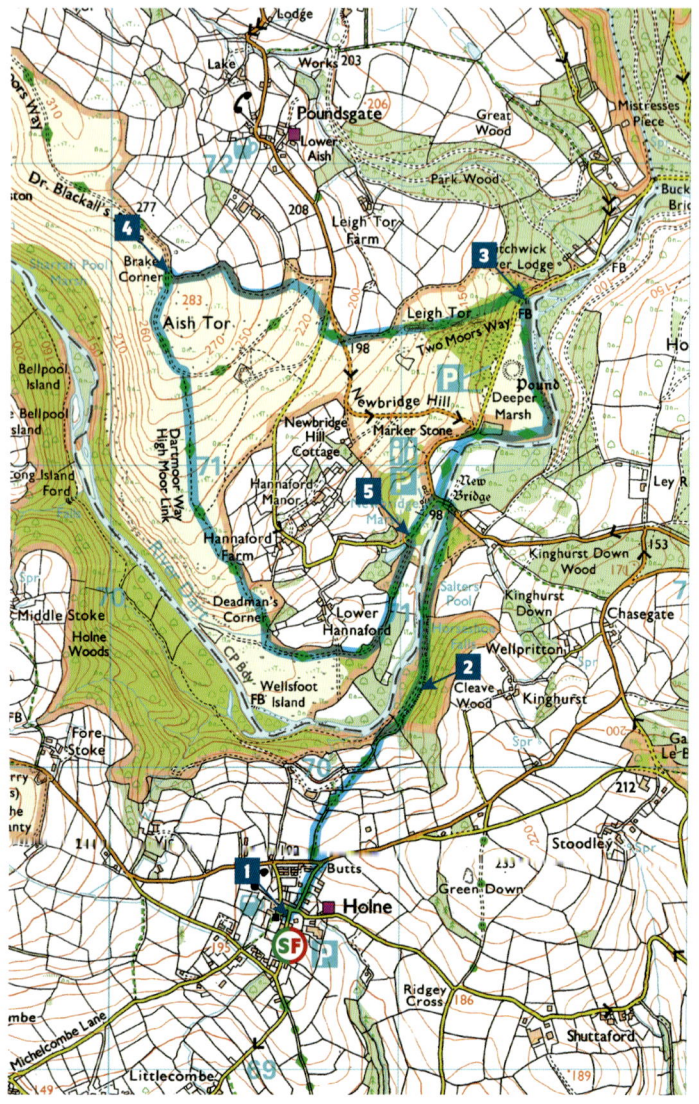

WALK 14 – HOLNE AND LEIGH TOR

1 Start at the village hall in **Holne** looking towards the church. The community shop and tea room is 50m to the left.

> Inside the Church of St Mary the Virgin is a magnificent early 16th-century carved pulpit and roodscreen painted with images of saints. In the churchyard is a yew tree that is reputedly over 1000 years old.

Turn right past the Church House Inn (left) to a crossroads. The route now follows the Two Moors Way to Leigh Tor. Cross straight over (signed to Ashburton and Princetown) and go up the lane to a T-junction. Turn left for 25m, then turn right and go through a gate (footpath to New Bridge). Follow the enclosed path downhill, cross a stile and bear half-right. Keep ahead down through fields and three kissing gates, then down through woodland to a signed junction.

2 Bear right, with the **River Dart** on your left. At a Y-junction, fork left and continue. Go through a gate, cross a footbridge and turn left to cross the 15th-century **New Bridge** over the River Dart. Immediately turn left towards Hannaford (car park and toilets on the right) and turn left again, following a signed path for Deeper Marsh under the bridge. Follow the path alongside the fence with the river

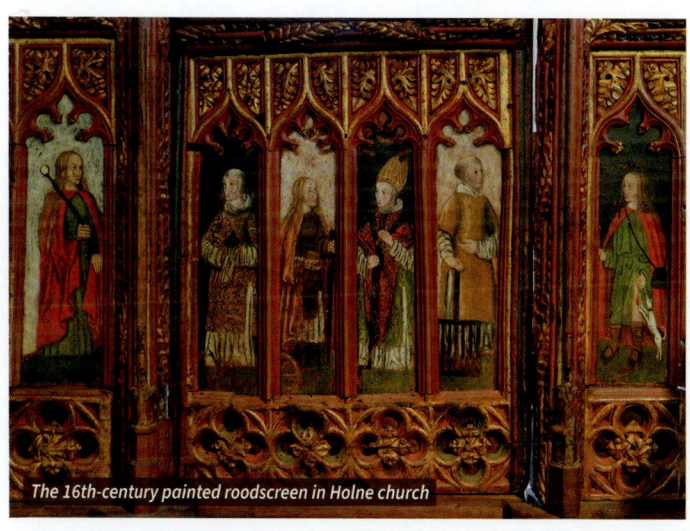
The 16th-century painted roodscreen in Holne church

Ancient yew tree in the churchyard at Holne

WALK 14 – HOLNE AND LEIGH TOR

on the right. Then head up beside a fence on the right before heading downhill. Now follow the River Dart through **Deeper Marsh**. Later, as the river swings right, bear left to a lane. Despite its name, Deeper Marsh is not marshy but an open, grassy area beside the River Dart, and is a well-known summer picnic spot.

3 Cross straight over and follow a zig-zag path steeply up through the trees, later passing just right of **Leigh Tor**. Keep ahead with a boundary on the right to a parking area. Cross straight over the road and continue to a lane. Turn right along this, then left into a car park. Take the path in the top right corner and continue up to a boundary wall. Turn left, following the wall uphill, passing over **Aish Tor**. At the wall corner bear right to join a track. The walk now follows the Dartmoor Way High Moor Link to New Bridge.

4 Turn left and follow the track known as **Dr Blackall's Drive** for 375m (6min), with Aish Tor on the left. The drive was constructed in the late 19th century for Dr Blackall, owner of Spitchwick Manor, so that he could drive his horse and carriage and enjoy the views. As the track curves left and starts descending, turn right at a marker post and Dartmoor Way sign to follow a narrow path down through the gorse. On approaching a boundary

The medieval New Bridge and the River Dart

The view from Dr Blackall's Drive

wall, bear right and continue down to a junction with a wide, level track. Turn left along this to a lane.

5 Bear right along the lane to a T-junction at **New Bridge** (car park and toilets on the left). Turn right across the bridge, then right across a footbridge and through a gate. Keep ahead to a signed Y-junction (Waypoint 2), fork left uphill and retrace the outward route back to **Holne**.

> ⓘ *The 173km-long Dartmoor Way visits many of the attractive towns and villages that nestle on the edge of Dartmoor. The 37km Dartmoor Way High Moor Link runs between Buckfastleigh and Tavistock.*

> **— To shorten**
> Split the walk into two shorter walks, one starting at Holne to New Bridge and back (3.5km, 1hr 15min) and a circular one starting at New Bridge (5km, 1hr 30min).

WALK 15
Ten Commandments Stone

Time 2hr
Distance 6.5km (4 miles)
Climb 165m

A walk of two halves – an easier walk to Buckland Beacon and a walk with more climbing up to Rippon Tor

Start/finish	Cold East Cross
Locate	///stall.lame.fits
Cafes/pubs	None on route
Transport	No public transport
Parking	Car park at Cold East Cross (TQ13 7JB)
Toilets	No public toilets on route

The first half of this route consists of a fairly level walk from Cold East Cross over Welstor Common to Buckland Beacon and The Ten Commandments Stone, then heads back over open moor to the car park. The second half heads up across Halshanger Common to Rippon Tor. After admiring the view, retrace your steps back down to Cold East Cross. The walk can easily be undertaken as two separate, shorter walks.

Looking back at the stone stile and sheep creep

SHORT WALKS DARTMOOR — SOUTH

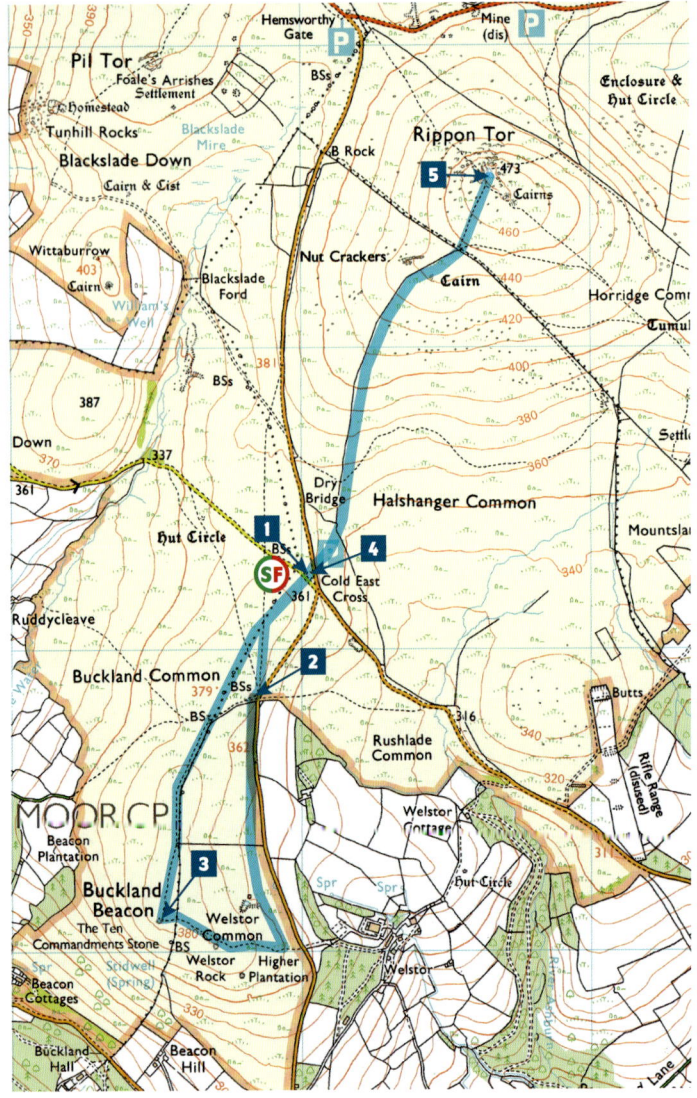

WALK 15 – TEN COMMANDMENTS STONE

1 Exit the car park and cross over the minor road, with the **Cold East Cross** junction to your left. Follow the grassy path opposite, gently up through the heather. At a junction (boundary stone) fork left towards a stand of trees located beside the road and small parking area. Keep to the right of the road and cross the stone stile in the wall beside the 'sheep creep' (a low hole in the wall).

2 After crossing the stile keep ahead on a grassy path and later pass through a disused gateway in an old boundary wall. Here the route splits – take the left fork and continue to a T-junction on **Welstor Common**. Turn right uphill, pass Welstor Rock (left) and cross the stile at the wall to arrive at **Buckland Beacon**. The Ten Commandments Stone is located on the left-hand side of the tor as you approach.

> **Views from Buckland Beacon include the Teign Estuary and coast (east), moving right is the South Hams region, then Brent Hill, to the west is Corndon Down, and to the north is Rippon Tor.**

3 Turn right, soon following the wall on your right. Where the wall turns right, go straight on (Rippon Tor is ahead). Keep ahead at two cross-junctions and pass three **boundary stones**, later retracing the outward route down to the minor road and car park.

The Ten Commandments Stone on Buckland Beacon

The gate leading to the path up Rippon Tor

4 Continue through the **car park**, cross another minor road and go through a gate in the wall opposite. Bear half-left and soon follow a boundary on your left up to a gate in the top left corner of **Halshanger Common**. Go through and keep ahead up to **Rippon Tor** (473m).

> Rippon Tor, crowned by Bronze Age burial cairns and a trig point, has some lovely views: look west to the TV mast at Princetown and moving right (clockwise) there is Hamel Down, further round is Hound Tor (north), Haytor Rocks (north-east), the Teign Estuary and coast (east), Buckland Beacon (south) and Brent Moor (south-west).

5 Turn around and retrace your steps back through the gate and down alongside the boundary which is on your right. Over to the right is a tor known as The Nutcrackers, which originally had a logan stone, or rocking stone. Once the boundary ends, bear half-right back to the gate in the wall and cross the minor road back to the **car park**.

WALK 15 – TEN COMMANDMENTS STONE

> ### – To shorten
> The walk can be split into two shorter walks, both starting from Cold East Cross: the Buckland Beacon loop (3km, 45m climbing, 50min) and Rippon Tor loop (3.5km, 120m climbing, 70min).

Buckland Beacon and The Ten Commandments Stone

Buckland Beacon is one of a chain of 16th-century beacons that were set up to warn of the arrival of the Spanish Armada out in the English Channel. On the southern side of the tor is The Ten Commandments Stone, two large granite slabs on which the Ten Commandments were carved by WA Clement in 1928. The work was commissioned by William Whitely, one-time Lord of Buckland Manor, to celebrate Parliament's rejection of a new Book of Common Prayer. Nearer the summit there is also a rather worn inscription commemorating King George V's Silver Jubilee in 1935.

View from Welstor Rock looking towards Buckland Beacon

The River Avon at Lydia Bridge (Walk 12)

USEFUL INFORMATION

Tourism bodies

Dartmoor National Park www.dartmoor.gov.uk

Visit Dartmoor www.visitdartmoor.co.uk

Tourist information centres

National Park Visitor Centres

Princetown, tel 01822 890414

Haytor, tel 0364 661520

Postbridge, tel 01822 880272

Travel

Train enquiries

National Rail www.nationalrail.co.uk

Bus timetables

Traveline www.traveline.info

Other contacts

Livestock incidents

All livestock, including ponies, are owned by local farmers and commoners. If you come across injured livestock please phone the Livestock Protection Officer, tel 07873 587561

Databases on Dartmoor tors and sites

The Tors of Dartmoor www.torsofdartmoor.co.uk

Dartefacts www.dartefacts.co.uk

© Steve Davison 2024
First edition 2024
ISBN: 978 1 78631 192 4
eISBN: 978 1 78765 134 0

MIX
Paper from responsible sources
FSC® C014138

Printed in Czechia on behalf of Latitude Press Ltd on responsibly sourced paper.
A catalogue record for this book is available from the British Library.
All photographs are by the author unless otherwise stated.

© Crown copyright 2024 OS AC0000810376

CICERONE

Cicerone Press, Juniper House, Murley Moss, Oxenholme Road, Kendal, Cumbria, LA9 7RL

www.cicerone.co.uk

Updates to this Guide

While every effort is made to ensure the accuracy of guidebooks as they go to print, changes can occur during the lifetime of an edition. Any updates that we know of for this guide will be on the Cicerone website (www.cicerone.co.uk/1192/updates), so please check before planning your trip. We also advise that you check information about transport, accommodation and shops locally. We are always grateful for updates, sent by email to updates@cicerone.co.uk or by post to Cicerone, Juniper House, Murley Moss, Oxenholme Road, Kendal, LA9 7RL.

Register your book: To sign up to receive free updates, special offers and GPX files where available, register your book at www.cicerone.co.uk.